Excelling With Autism:
Obtaining Critical Mass
Using Deliberate Practice

An Evidence-Based Approach

Brenda Smith Myles, PhD

Kerry Mataya, MS

Hollis Shaffer

FUTURE HORIZONS

817.277.0727
817.277.2270 (fax)
email: info@fhautism.com
www.fhautism.com

©2018 Brenda Smith Myles

ISBN: 978-1-942197-38-6

TABLE OF CONTENTS

Developing Specific Goals

Ensuring Focus

Assisting the Learner to Move Out of Comfort Zone

Communicating Outcomes

INTRODUCTION TO CRITICAL MASS

I think the teaching profession contributes more to the future of our society than any other single profession.
– John Wooden

It is now widely recognized that the potential of individuals with autism spectrum disorder (ASD) is unlimited. For example, the nonverbal 3-year-old may become a successful college student, a plumber, IT specialist, grocery bagger, social worker, movie theater ticket taker, parent, aunt, spouse, etc. Further, it is important to understand that the behaviors we see at any given time in no way determine potential.

Those who teach and support learners with ASD play an essential role in helping individuals with ASD achieve life success. *Teachers* – we use that term here to mean anyone who provides instruction and supports in a systematic and mindful manner – are responsible for facilitating the learning of individuals with ASD by selecting instructional goals, teaching and supporting strategically, and determining how to measure progress.

This is a tremendous responsibility! Errors in any of these functions – often due to administrative demands, financial constraints, and legislative mandates – may limit the potential of individuals on the spectrum and, as a result, may impact their quality of life throughout adulthood.

This book introduces a new way to optimize the progress of learners on the spectrum by viewing instruction and supports from a novel perspective.

Ultimately, we want everybody – including those with ASD – to be able to move about their world as independently as possible, making informed decisions about their wants and needs, and have a high quality of life. We want everybody – including those with ASD – to be successful, not only with tasks and activities they have been taught to do, but also with tasks and activities that they have not received instruction on.

In other words, we want everyone to be able to create their own knowledge based on their experiences and apply it flexibly to novel situations. This is called *critical mass*. Think of critical mass as true mastery of a skill. Critical mass, in this sense, is the point where an individual has gained enough information to be successful in situations, activities, or skills for which instruction has not been provided.

> Critical mass originated in the study of physics, then served as a way to study organic chemical changes, animal behavior, and, most recently, human collective behavior. It is a socio-dynamic term that is used to describe the existence of sufficient momentum such that momentum becomes self-sustaining and creates further growth (Oliver, Marwell, & Teixeira, 1985).

Within education, critical mass may be thought of as a burst of new behavior or behaviors that happen after a learner has received sufficient instruction and experiences in a related topic or area. Critical mass may also be thought of as the *tipping point* –the time where, after instruction and multiple experiences, momentum takes over and the learner can apply the information, behavior or skills[1] in multiple new ways (Blum, 2017; Gladwell, 2002). As such, *critical mass can be thought of as spontaneous generalization.*

Adapted from Munch, C. (2010, November 22). Pushing an online business to gain momentum. Retrieved June 16, 2017 from http://munchweb.com/the-tipping-point.

---

[1] The terms, "information," "behavior," and "skills," as they relate to critical are used interchangeably throughout this book.

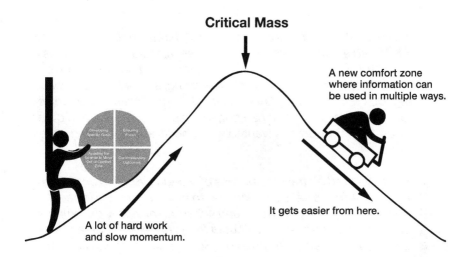

Critical mass is not just about developing habits and routines, nor is it rote memory. It means having the ability to take known information and using it in both new and similar situations.

> Critical mass has increasingly been seen as a universal concept, equally applicable to water and magnets as to animals and humans. Today, the study of critical mass is central to almost all discussions of behavior and norms because the dynamics of system change are remarkably constant across disciplines (Worster, 2013, p. 7).

Critical mass can occur across groups of people, animals, or objects. This book does not address this type of critical mass. Rather, it focuses on attaining critical mass of knowledge and skills in an *individual*. Critical mass, for the purposes of this book, occurs when behaviors are taught and deliberately practiced so that growth in similar skills will occur without instruction (Rogers, 2003).

Critical mass, in this regard, occurs

- When you have accumulated enough experiences shopping at grocery stores in your community to realize that you could go into almost any grocery store in the country and have a successful shopping experience. You are also confident that you could go to a shopping mall or a hardware store or boutique because there will be similarities – these are all shopping venues where you select what you want from categorized items.

- When you are comfortable going to your first B&B because you have experienced hotels and you know there will be some overlap in the two environments.

As an adult, Suzan, a 50ish woman with high-functioning ASD (HF-ASD), had an opportunity to travel to several state conferences on ASD. She was always accompanied by a friend because she found airports and hotels confusing, exhausting, and anxiety-provoking. Despite having an IQ in the gifted range, Suzan saw airports as separate entities that had nothing in common with each other. Thus, every airport she went to was a novel and unsettling experience.

Suzan wanted air travel to be less of a cognitive drain and asked for help. A friend sat down with her to help her develop specific goals for mastering air travel and subsequently provided support and feedback so that Suzan could focus on relevant details and screen out irrelevant information. Suzan and her friend knew that Suzan would have to move outside her comfort zone, so they worked together to ensure that she had the supports in place to make this learning experience as painless as possible. As Suzan practiced, she made occasional errors, but she continued to refine her process until traveling through airports became almost second nature to her. She required no support to use bus transit as she had reached critical mass in transit.

Why Did We Write This Book?

The answer is simple – most individuals with ASD are not reaching their potential. For example, the unemployment rate for those on the spectrum is higher than for any other disability group because they often do not reach mastery of pivotal skills that would allow them to utilize those skills flexibly in order to be successfully independent – they do not reach critical mass.

60% of young adults with ASD never worked for pay into their early twenties compared to 99% of their typically developing peers. Rates of independent living are also abysmal – 81% live with family members or caregivers. And this is consistent across the spectrum – from those who have a classic presentation of ASD to those who have average-to-above-average IQs (Roux, Shattuck, Rast, Rava, & Anderson, 2015).

This should be a wake-up call to do things differently. And that is what this book is about – doing things differently to positively impact individuals on the spectrum by supporting the development of critical mass in areas that are necessary for successful functioning in home, work, and community.

CHAPTER 1: INTRODUCTION TO CRITICAL MASS

Critical mass happens naturally for some people; for others, support is needed. In schools in the United States, the majority of students with average or higher cognitive ability achieve critical mass in subjects such as reading and basic math skills. This is by design, because these skills are considered to be so essential that a massive amount of direct instruction is provided. Multiple lessons on these topics are presented year after year. Hundreds and thousands of hours of drill and practice on math and reading are built into the educational system. The result is critical mass. That is, most students gain reading skills that allow them to generalize across reading materials – instructions for assembling a bookshelf, news on Facebook, texts on phones, recipes from the Internet, and so forth. Most students can use these basic reading skills with ease and confidence. The same occurs with basic math skills.

The majority of neurotypical (NT) students also gain critical mass in the areas of social, communication, and basic living skills. This is not attributable to the curriculum of the schools. It occurs through implicit learning – that is, without instruction. NT students begin to make friends, hold conversations, and become aware of fashion and grooming without formal lessons and without years of drill and practice. Motivation for this type of learning is "built in," and reinforcement for successful practice occurs naturally, leading to competence. In general, therefore NT students leave high school with enough social, communication, and basic living skills to enable them to generalize these abilities to employment, postsecondary training, and independent living.

Students with HF-ASD, on the other hand, have a different experience. For the most part, with good instruction, they, too, develop critical mass in the areas of reading and basic math. They are able to take these skills and apply them in multiple settings for varied uses. In short, they have benefited from the explicit instruction that the education system provides in these areas.

But in vast contrast, students with HF-ASD have not gained the social, communication, and daily living skills necessary for successful further education, employment, and independent living because they are not able (unlike their NT cohorts) to gain these skills through implicit learning (Schipul & Just, 2016), and schools have not provided sufficient explicit instruction in these areas. These students will never meet critical mass in social, communication and daily living skills if they do not receive direct instruction – multiple lessons presented year after year.

> Why do students with ASD have difficulty learning implicitly? Because they have a different neurology (Hazlett et al., 2017). Very simply, most individuals with ASD are "wired" to learn from direct or explicit instruction (Stoner et al., 2014) and, therefore, must be explicitly taught what others learn by themselves. That is, what others learn implicitly in terms of social, communication, and daily living skills can develop in individuals with ASD only after enough explicit instruction as well as deliberate practice has occurred.

How Do Learners With ASD Fare in Areas That They Do Not Learn Implicitly, Specifically Social Interactions?

Compared to the interactions of their NT peers, almost no students on the spectrum are taught to attain critical mass when it comes to social skills. Research tells us that, students with HF-ASD have fewer opportunities to practice these skills, let alone opportunities to engage in deliberate practice under the guidance of a teacher or mentor.

For example, in their study of the social interactions of kindergarten children, Jahr, Eikeseth, Eldevik, and Aase (2007) found that the mean frequency of interaction during one hour of free play was 90% of the time for NT children compared to 31% for students with HF-ASD.

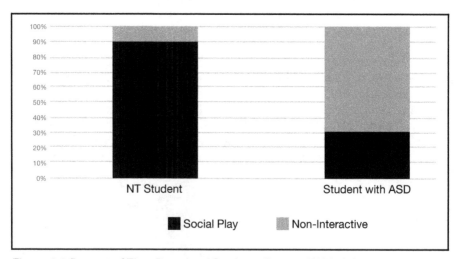

Figure 1.1. Percent of Time Preschool Students Engaged With Others

CHAPTER 1: INTRODUCTION TO CRITICAL MASS

During a One-Hour Playtime. *Jahr, Eikeseth, Eldevik, & Aase (2007)*

To illustrate, let's look at the social interaction opportunities of kindergarten children with HF-ASD vs. those of their NT peers during full-day kindergarten with one hour of playtime or recess each day.

Using the above data, an NT child would engage with others for 54 minutes during play time, whereas a child with HF-ASD would spend 19 minutes interacting with others. *Over the course of a 180-day school year, this would translate into the NT child having 162 hours of social interaction practice during play, whereas the child with HF-ASD would have 57 hours – almost a third less.*

Let's apply this to *all* of the elementary school years (first through fifth grade), where students typically spend 30 minutes per day in unstructured social settings, such as recess and lunch. Across first through fifth grade, NT students would spend a total of *567* hours in social practice whereas students with HF-ASD would spend a total of *202* hours similarly engaged – again, less than half. This does not take into consideration social interactions that occur after school or on weekends, where it well documented that children and youth with HF-ASD have fewer opportunities to interact (Jahr, et al., 2017). *In short, those who need the most practice, receive the least.*

In another study focused on how preschool children with HF-ASD spent playtime, Gunn, Trembath, and Hudry (2014) reported that preschool children with HF-ASD spent 89% of playtime in solitary play, 8% in parallel play, and 3% in interactive play. Hestenes and Carroll (2000) found a different pattern for typically developing peers – solitary play: 16%; parallel play: 16%, and interactive play: 68%. *Again, those who need the most practice – students with HF-ASD – receive the least.*

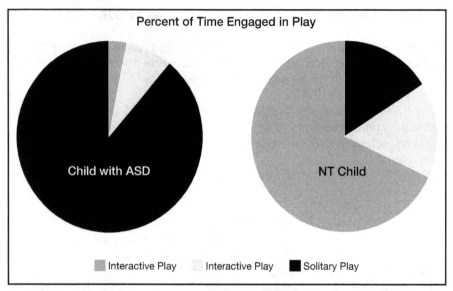

Figure 1.2. A Comparison of Play Formats for Preschool Children with ASD and Their NT Peers (estimated). *Hestenes & Carroll (2000)*

What is worse, these deficits in practice persist throughout the lives of individuals with HF-ASD. For example, Orsmond and Kuo (2011) looked at with whom adolescents with HF-ASD spend their time, defined as recreational or social activities. A total of 73% of their free time was spent with or in the presence of family or paid professionals (i.e., providers), 9% with peers, and 18% alone. No differences were found between the school year and summer vacation.

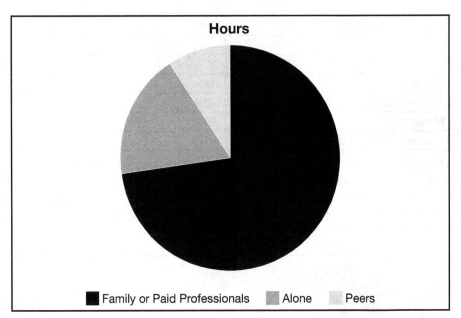

Figure 1.3. Companions for Adolescents with ASD During Free Time. *Orsmond & Kuo (2011)*

Further, Orsmond and Kuo (2011) identified the types of activities in which adolescents with HF-ASD engaged. As shown in Table 1.1, a mere 15% spent time having a conversation with others. The remaining 85% spent no time in conversation during their daily lives.

Table 1.1
Percent of Adolescents With ASD Who Engage in Free-Time Activities

Activity	Percent Who Spent Time Engaged in Activity
Watching television	86%
Using computer	53%
Engaging in physical activity	47%

Listening to music	45%
Shopping	44%
Relaxing (unoccupied)	36%
Reading	36%
Visiting with friends and relatives	20%
Napping	15%
Having a conversation	15%

These patterns of limited or no social interactions appear to hold true for most individuals with HF-ASD across the lifespan. For example, Roux et al. (2015) reported limited social participation of adults with ASD, including 69% and 54%, who reported that they never saw friends and were not invited to social activities, respectively.

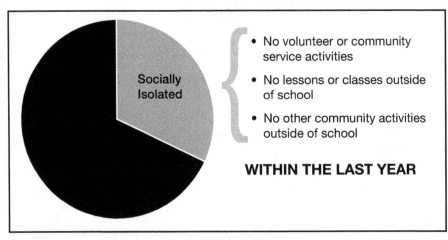

Figure 1.4. Community Participation of Young Adults with ASD. *Roux et al., 2015*

While it is impossible to know for sure, it is plausible that the failure to provide opportunities for practice of social skills has dire results, including higher rates of unemployment and incarceration. The same can be said of communication skills and daily living skills – important, not directly taught to a level of competence, and have a lifelong impact.

With regard to employment, Agran, Hughes, Thoma, and Scott (2016) found that social and communication skills rank high among the factors that are valued by potential employers. Table 1.2 provides a list of skills essential to successful employment and the frequency of instruction of these skills. Even when these skills are included in a curriculum, the opportunity to amass the necessary hours of deliberate practice is not provided.

Table 1.2
Employment-Related Social Skills

Employment Social Skill	Importance	Instruction Frequency
Seeks clarification	1	8
Arrives at work on time	2	6
Refrains from touching others	3	19
Carries out instructions needing immediate attention	4	10
Notifies supervisor when assistance is needed	5	16
Responds appropriately to critical feedback	6	14
Interacts well with customers/clients	7	9
Responds appropriately to job-related emergencies	8	27
Works as a member of a team, when appropriate	9	11
Finds necessary information prior to performing a job	10	18
Listens without interrupting	11	4
Works at job continuously without disruptions	12	12
Uses appropriate conversational skills	13	3
Shows initiative	14	7
Acknowledges what others say	15	2
Solves problems	16	5
Uses non-objectionable language or gestures	17	22
Works at rates compatible with company expectations	18	20
Does not argue with coworkers	19	28
Uses social niceties ("please," "thank you")	20	1
Uses valid excuses for lateness or absence	21	24
Refers others to those who are qualified to carry out tasks, as appropriate	22	23
Carries out instructions in a timely manner	23	26
Offers help	24	13
Demonstrates appropriate affect (most of the time)	25	15
Expresses appreciation to coworkers	26	17
Does not talk to coworkers instead of working	27	21
Provides job-related information to other employees	28	25
Does not talk about personal problems at inappropriate times	29	29
Does not have friends around during work hours	30	30

From Agran, M., Hughes, C., Thoma, C. A., & Scott, L. A. (2016). Employment social skills: What skills are really valued. *Career Development and Transition for Exceptional Individuals, 39*(2), 111-120.

Further, with regard to incarceration, involvement of individuals with HF-

ASD in the judiciary system is of high concern. Thus, the incarceration rate of individuals with ASD is four times greater than the rate of ASD in the general population (Fazio, Pietz, & Denney, 2012).

In fact, Michna and Trestman (2016) suggest that the high rate of incarceration for individuals with ASD is possibly linked to challenges that would be lessened with greater access to practice social and communication skills. For example, acts of aggression that may lead to incarceration sometimes result from misinterpretation of others' behavior. This misinterpretation may have been avoided had deliberate practice been provided.

> "Although commonly present in early childhood, symptoms may not fully manifest until social demands exceed the capacity of the individual to cope. As the individual with ASD ages, odd behaviors accepted in childhood may be seen as threatening or unwelcome in adulthood" (Michna & Trestman, 2016, p. 253).

How Do We Support Individuals With HF-ASD to Achieve Critical Mass?

We provide deliberate practice. Ericsson (2016), a Swedish psychologist, wrote about the role of deliberateness in reaching a high level of competence. Ericsson has made a career of identifying the elements necessary to create expert performance in areas such as chess, world class gymnastics, memory, and laproscopic surgery.

According to Ericsson (2016), there are four components of deliberate practice, each accomplished under the guidance of an expert coach, such as a teacher or mentor:

- Developing specific goals
- Ensuring focus
- Communicating outcomes
- Assisting the learner to move out of his or her comfort zone.

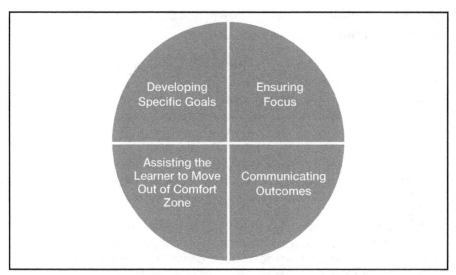

Figure 1.5. The elements of deliberate practice. *Adapted from Ericsson & Pool, 2017*

We know how to use these components to enhance explicitly learned skills for individuals with a typical neurology. What if we applied the same elements to individuals with HF-ASD, focusing on skills that others implicitly learn and extensively practice?

> Ericsson says, "So imagine what might be possible with efforts that are inspired and directed by a clear scientific understanding of the best ways to build expertise. And imagine what might be possible if we applied the techniques that have proved to be so effective in sports and music and chess to all the different types of learning that people do ...?" (2016, p. 10).

We, in turn, say, imagine what might be possible if these techniques were harnessed to help those with HF-ASD. Imagine if the elements of deliberate practice were built into the educational system to help these individuals learn social, communication, and daily living skills – skills implicitly mastered by NT students.

Summary

We want everyone – including those with HF-ASD – to be able to create their own knowledge based on their experiences and apply it flexibly to novel situations. Achieving critical mass is powerful. When you reach critical mass on a topic or experience ...

The way you think about a topic or experience can change, and that thinking may be applied to new situations:

- Confidence in being able to perform in somewhat similar or even novel situations is likely to increase
- The ability to retain information improves
- The ability to problem-solve will be enhanced (Worster, 2013).

Because we have not yet fully incorporated the concept of critical mass into instruction, the potential of individuals with HF-ASD is not realized in home, school, and community. Most do not live independently, are un- or underemployed, and engage in few social interactions, resulting in isolation. To change this trajectory, we need to do things differently. We need to teach skills in a way that will lead to critical mass. Without critical mass in areas that are implicitly learned by their NT peers, individuals with ASD will continue to be excluded from positive outcomes in postsecondary education and training, employment, and lifelong independent living.

Deliberate practice in a given area leads to success, and although we do not know precisely how many practice opportunities an individual needs to reach critical mass, it is widely agreed that *more practice is better*. No study in the field of education has identified the number of practice opportunities necessary to promote critical mass because every individual and situation is unique.

> One study, outside of education, attempted to determine how much "practice" is needed to create a new ability – that is, for critical mass to occur. To improve its understanding of language, Google fed its artificial intelligence (AI) engine romance novels. To learn to write one novel, the computer had to "digest" 2,865 romance novels (Ghoshal, 2016).

Students with HF-ASD are capable of reaching critical mass, but they do so differently than their NT counterparts. They require deliberate practice – an enormous amount of practice – in topics that are both explicitly and implicitly learned by NT learners. That is, they need deliberate practice in academic areas as well as communication, social, and daily living skills.

Imagine what might be possible if we applied the techniques of deliberate practice to help individuals with HF-ASD learn skills that are implicitly mastered by others, including social, communication, and daily living skills. Would this result in our learners attaining critical mass?

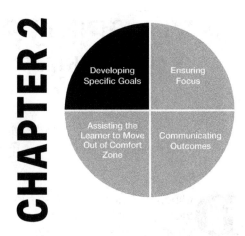

CHAPTER 2

This book discusses those elements of deliberate practice that must be in place for critical mass to occur, including

- Developing specific and meaningful goals
- Ensuring focus
- Communicating outcomes
- Assisting the learner to move out of the comfort zone

Throughout this book, these concepts are further explained using examples from various areas of science, including neuroscience, psychology, biology, medicine, and meteorology. This will allow readers to understand the impact of critical mass – not only on individuals with ASD – but to the world.

The final chapter points out how deliberate practice relates to The Individuals with Disabilities Education Act (2004) as defined by a recent Supreme Court case.

DEVELOPING SPECIFIC AND MEANINGFUL GOALS

If you don't know where you're going,
you might not get there. **– Yogi Berra**

Deliberate practice requires a long-term commitment to a meaningful goal. It includes strategically identifying skills to teach and creating goals with the intention to improve student performance (cf. Huitt, 2011; Locke, Shaw, Saari, & Latham, 1981). If we want a student to be independent, we develop goals that ensure that the student can complete independently a task or activity from beginning to end.

The educational community typically develops such goals for academic skills, such as math. As a result, most students leave school able to apply math to balancing a checkbook, cooking, setting an alarm clock, determining when to leave home to get to work on time, and so forth. Further, typically developing students take this information and use it in novel ways, such as applying math principles to determine the amount of income tax they owe the IRS or how many pairs of shorts they need to take on a vacation.

But few instructional programs consistently develop meaningful goals that allow students with HF-ASD to learn and practice new skills so that they can be used independently in areas impacted by the autism neurology – social, communication, and daily living skills. True, individualized education programs (IEP) and lesson plans may include goals in these areas, but these skills are seldom taught so that the student can use them independently and in situations in which instruction has not occurred. Thus, it is important to determine what to teach by developing meaningful goals, including skills not implicitly learned by those on the spectrum. These goals should be taught using evidence-based practices (EBP) incorporating categorization and the levels of learning (Hodgetts & Park, 2017).

It is ideal to use all of these elements – EBP, categorization, and levels of learning – together; however, that can be overwhelming and difficult to do because of time, personnel, and curricular restraints. Start where you can. Using one element of deliberate practice until you can easily integrate it into the student's day is a great way to start.

Specific and meaningful goals take into account students' previous challenges, successes, and skill mastery. Goal setting and subsequent instruction should begin where previous instruction left off. If goals are not progressively changing, then critical mass will not be reached.

Determine What to Teach

Many learners with ASD have uneven skill development compared to their age group. For example, a student may be proficient with college-level reading material yet not have the central coherence – ability to discern relevant and irrelevant details – to follow the group discussion in his seventh-grade language arts class. This type of discrepancy requires the instructor and the learner to more carefully assess what the learner does and does not know.

Understand Evidence-Based Practices

Over the past several years, we have been witness to attempts to quantify effectiveness in almost every realm. Triggered, in part, by federal and state governments and funding agencies as a means of assessing accountability, the term *evidence-based* has been applied to multiple entities, including medicine, management, mental health, and education.

> EBP means there is research to show an intervention or activity is effective when implemented with fidelity.

The same focus has been directed to instructional programming for students with ASD. Many interventions exist to support individuals with ASD; yet, scientific research has found that only some of them are evidence-based (Wong et al., 2015). Three reports have attempted to identify EBPs for children and youth with ASD: The National Professional Development Center on ASD (NPDC on ASD, 2009, 2015), the National Autism Center (NAC, 2009, 2015), and the Centers for Medicare and Medicaid Services (CMS, 2010) each independently conducted reviews of the literature to identify effective interventions for individuals with ASD. Each created a set of specific criteria by which to identify interventions and supports as EBP.

Table 2.1 lists interventions identified as effective in the NPDC, NAC, and CMS reports. Because one of the three documents used different intervention terminology and descriptions, specific wording from each report is included so that the reader can determine the level of overlap among the reports. Briefly, EBP include strategies such as video modeling, visual supports, social skills training, and functional behavior assessments. Some strategies overlap.

Problems exist in the application of EBPs. For example, social communication intervention, social skills packages, and social skills training have been identified as EBP. Does that mean that any social communication intervention is effective? Can you select a social skills curriculum and count on it to include best practices?

Unfortunately, just because a social skills curriculum exists does not mean that it is effective. Many curricula are not supported by anecdotal reports or quantitative research. In light of limited guidance on effectiveness of specific materials, how will we know if such a curriculum is effective? The answer is: We take data! Resources such as *Taming the Data Monster: Collecting and Analyzing Classroom Data to Improve Student Progress* (Reeve & Cabot, 2015) and *Show Me the Data: Data-based Instructional Decisions Made Simple and Easy* (Leon-Geurrero, Matsumoto, & Martin, 2011) can be helpful in developing data collection systems.

All in all, we are looking for ways to best help learners with ASD to manipulate, retrieve, and store information efficiently. EBPs are essential in providing instruction to reach critical mass when they are used with fidelity. That is, those who use EBPs must explicitly follow the guidelines specified in the research literature.

Table 2.1

Evidence-based Practices Identified by the Centers for Medicare and Medicaid Services (CMS), National Autism Center (NAC), and the National Professional Development Center (NPDC)

EBP	CMS		NAC		NPDC	
	Elementary	Secondary	Elementary	Secondary	Elementary	Secondary
Antecedent-based interventions	X	X	X	X	X	X

					Video modeling	Video modeling
Behavioral package	X					
• Differential reinforcement			X	X	X	X
• Extinction					X	X
• Reinforcement					X	X
• Discrete trial training					X	
• Time delay					X	X
• Response interruption redirection					X	
• Naturalistic teaching strategies					X	
• Picture Exchange Communication System					X	
• Pivotal Response Training					X	
• Comprehensive behavioral package			X			
• Cognitive behavioral package	X				X	
• Functional behavior assessment	X				X	
• Functional communication training					X	X
• Task analysis						X
Exercise				X	X	
Joint attention intervention	X	X				
Modeling	X	X	X	Video modeling	Video modeling	Video modeling

Multi-component package	X			X	
Parent-implemented interventions					
Peer-implemented interventions	X	X		X	X
Self-management	X	X	X	X	X
• Social interventions	X			X	X
• Social communication intervention	X			X	
• Social skills package	X			X	
• Social skills training	X			X	X
• Structured plan groups	X			X	X
Social narratives/Story-based intervention package	X	X		X	
Structured teaching	X				
• Schedules	X	X		X	
• Visual supports	X				
Technology-based treatment/technology aided instruction and intervention	X			X	X

- Takes over any responsibilities that he perceives other group members are not competent to do.
- Becomes distressed if someone writes too firmly on his paper making a scraping noise.
- Cannot agree with group members in selecting a topic.
- Interrupts others without the awareness that someone else is talking.
- Cannot acknowledge that others have good ideas.
- Spends an inordinate amount of time on a minor detail, such as selecting a computer font for a report.
- And so on ...

Table 2.2 provides a list of concepts beyond academics that must be learned. Although not a comprehensive list, it may be useful in determining skills that are necessary in adult life. If the student has not learned and practiced these skills, he will not be able to be employed in *any* venue in which people must work together.

Table 2.2
Sample of Skills That Facilitate Life Success

Adaptability	Negotiation
Asking for help	Observation
Assertive communication	Organization of materials
Attention	Patience
Attribution	Persistence
Categorization	Perspective taking
Cause and effect	Positive thinking
Central coherence	Prioritizing
Change	Problem solving
Collaboration	Regulation
Compromise	Role model
Confidence	Safety
Conflict resolution	Seeking information
Conversation	Self-analysis
Curiosity and questions	Self-control and staying calm
Daily living skills	Self-determination
Delegating	Self-awareness
Emotional connection	Sequencing
Emotional understanding	Social judgment
Enjoyment	Stamina
Executive function	Task analysis
Flexibility	Task completion
Follow through	Teamwork
Goal setting	Theory of mind
Hidden curriculum	Time management
Inhibition	Using resources
Interdependence	Waiting
Internal motivation	Willingness to learn
Listening	Work ethic

Each of these skills is important, but they must be prioritized so neither the instructor nor the learner becomes overwhelmed. Use the results of standardized and informal assessments, teacher and parent concerns and preferences, learner interests and concerns, and team discussion as resources to help you identify what to teach first.

The best way to develop skills is to provide high levels of support at first and then fade some supports as the student displays elements of the new skill (see page 54). Too often, the supports that have been put in place are never faded or the learner does not know how to use the supports independently, leaving her without the ability to use a skill on her own. Thus, critical mass is never reached. This does not mean that all supports should be faded. For example, calendar and organizational supports should always be in place. These supports are and should be used as independently as possible by almost everyone to track and meet time requirements and demands.

Do not underestimate the impact of attaining critical mass. From critical mass emerges new skills. For example, many skills within a game of baseball can be learned to the point of critical mass. When this occurs, similar skills, rules, and interactions can be automatically applied to other ball-related activities such as kickball, because of previous experience with running bases, and wall ball, because of previous experience with throwing. That's the beauty of critical mass. Again, critical mass, for the purposes of this book, occurs when skills are taught and practiced sufficiently so that growth in similar skills will occur without instruction (Rogers, 2003).

Using Categorization

We have chosen to separate categorization from the skills discussed above because of its importance in developing critical mass. Categorization can be thought of as an early problem-solving skill.

Categorization is used to describe the relationship and differences among subjects, topics, ideas, objects, etc. Evident within the first year of life when babies begin to identify similarities and differences, categorization is fundamental to developing and using language, predicting, making inferences, making decisions and interacting with others and the environment (cf. Walker & Gopnik, 2014). It is critically important because the ability to categorize allows new information to be integrated with known material and organized in a manageable way reducing demands on memory and allowing an individual to focus on important aspects of objects (cf. Gastgeb, Dundas, Minshew, & Strauss, 2012).

Categories help us work toward goals, such as recalling a list of items or solving a problem (cf. Alderson-Day & McGonigle-Chalmer, 2011). In addition, categories help re-identify objects, places, animals, and so forth, over time and assist in determining what elements within a category are relevant, irrelevant, a certainty, or typically occurring (Walker & Gopnik, 2014). Very simply, the ability to categorize is one of the basic building blocks of social bonding, language learning, and the development of general life skills (Gastgeb et al., 2012).

Most of us develop categories implicitly, but learners on the spectrum do not (cf. Alderson-Day & McGonigle-Chalmer, 2011; Fiebelkorn, Foxe, McCourt, Dumas, & Molholm, 2013). EEGs reveal those with ASD differ from their NT peers in their ability to determine which items do and do not belong to specific categories (Fiebelkorn et al., 2013). This means that they function in a world where each item is new. For example, Temple Grandin (1995) says that before she learned to categorize, she processed each dog she saw as unique and did not group them as "dogs."

Table 2.3 shows an example of how to categorize elements related to a picnic: place, people, food, and weather.

Table 2.3

Elements and Examples of a Picnic

Place	People	Food	Weather
Park on the ground	Immediate family	Fried chicken	Sunny
Backyard on a picnic table	Neighbors	Peanut butter and jelly sandwiches	Cloudy
Classroom on the floor	Classmates	Lunchroom food	Rainy

(Personal communication, Bock, 2000)

This table shows just a few examples of a picnic. Understanding the categories of the picnic and its multiple exemplars or examples allows us to create numerous variations of picnics and move with from one to another rather than assuming there is only one type of picnic.

> One of our friends with HF-ASD experienced some social challenges when she told a newly hired colleague that she didn't want any more booty calls from him. Her attempts to categorize the words that identify accidental phone calls (i.e., pocket dials, butt dial) resulted in this error.

Even if an item is recognized by most people as falling within a specific category, it may be miscategorized by the student with ASD, disrupting recall (Fields, 2012) and preventing the learner from using the information in a flexible way.

> Consider the picnic example from the perspective from a student with HF-ASD, Henrik. Henrik and his class are going on a picnic. Henrik's teacher prepares the class for the outing by showing them a picture of the nearby park where they will eat and providing the picnic menu. They go to the park with a picnic basket of sandwiches, chips, vegetables, apples, and water. The class occupies the picnic benches in the park and Henrik enjoys the outing.

> Upon hearing from Henrik that he enjoyed the picnic, his parents plan a similar outing. Sadly, Henrik had a meltdown when this "picnic" happened in Henrik's backyard, sitting

on the ground with a menu of fried chicken and "fixins" from one of the family's favorite restaurants.

Why did he melt down? Henrik did not understand that a picnic consisted of elements from a set of categories. He interpreted picnic literally – to mean his exact experience from the school picnic.

Categorization is more than a skill to teach separately. It is so important that it must be integrated into instruction of every new skill. Bock (1994, 1999, 2001, 2007) has successfully taught various skills using categorization, including laundry sortings, stocking shelves in a grocery store, noun and verb endings, and social interaction skills.

Develop Specific Goals Using the Levels of Learning

Even if social, communication, and daily living skills are addressed in a student's instructional program, they are largely not taught and practiced systematically to the point of automaticity. Comfortable with some gains, intervention teams may overlook teaching skills to the level that they can be used independently. However, such a "partial" approach to intervention will have negative long-term outcomes. It does not promote growth as evidenced by a lack of progress on goals; lack of generalization of skills; and over-dependence on assistance, modifications, and accommodations (Aspy & Grossman, 2011).

Too often, calendar and organization systems, for example, are limited to the education setting in which they have been practiced without teaching a calendar system that would work or be available throughout the student's life. To change this, students with ASD often have to be explicitly taught to find and purchase a calendar during the middle and high school years rather than just being handed one. Once the student has received direct instruction on the need for a calendar and how to pick out a calendar, he is more likely to develop critical mass in this area to generalize this skill into life after high school. This includes critical mass in buying a calendar by shopping at any store or looking through any calendars to find one that is the right fit. If this skill is not explicitly taught, it does not occur to some students that a calendar should be purchased and used after high school.

In order to maximize instructional time and provide appropriate instruction for students with HF-ASD, teachers must determine the instructional readiness level for each skill to be taught. Specifically, a student's level of learning must be matched to appropriate goals and instructional procedures in order to provide instruction that will increase learning. Thus, an understanding of levels of learning, or levels of skill acquisition, is necessary to enhance the student's learning. When the levels of learning are integrated into instruction, you help ensure that students systematically learn a skill from start to finish – introduction to interdependence.

> We use the term "interdependence" purposefully. Those who support and love individuals with ASD want them to be independent. Goals and benchmarks are written around independence and it is held as the highest level of skill development. Is this what we want for individuals with ASD? Perhaps not. Neurotypical people (NT) are not independent. They are interdependent. That is, NTs are mutually reliant on each other. They know what they can do themselves, they know what they need help with, and they know how to seek out that help.

Hudson, Colson, and Braxdale (1984) introduced the levels-of-learning model. This does not merely contain a list of how students learn or process information; it aids teachers in developing goals and instructional programs for learners with ASD and ensures that skills are learned from start to finish. The six levels of learning are (a) awareness, (b) recognition, (c) recall, (d) application, (e) generalization, and (d) maintenance (see Figure 2.1).

Maintenance

Generalization

Application

Recall

Recognition

Awareness

Figure 2.1. Levels of Learning. *Hudson, Colson, & Braxdale (1984)*

Awareness

Awareness is the necessary first step to learning any new skill or concept. You cannot learn about something if you do not know that it exists. Once the student is aware of an item or concept, he is prepared to learn to include that item in his environment. In addition, a student can be aware something is happening, but not see why it is a problem. It is important for someone to have awareness of what is happening and why it is a problem. For example, a learner with HF-ASD will not be successful in interpreting facial expressions, until he realizes that (a) facial expressions exist, (b) they have meaning and (c) similar expressions may have various meanings.

> *Jose, a 16-year-old with HF-ASD, described being surprised to learn that a fake smile does not mean that someone is happy. Until he knew that, he assumed that his classmates were his friends and their fake smile was a true smile.*

Recognition

At the recognition level, the student demonstrates that she can discriminate target item(s) from distractors. In addition, the student may be able to complete a task with the assistance of a model. For example, at this level, the student can discriminate a happy from a sad face when presented with a visual and two options (happy/sad) from which to choose.

> *When Jose reaches the recognition level, he can match an emotion word to a face, such as matching annoyed to a fake smile, or correctly discern the correct response from multiple options such as pictures of a happy smile versus an annoyed smile.*

Recall

Following mastery at the recognition level, the student progresses to the recall level. At this stage, the student independently retrieves information. The student can freely answer questions without being provided with response options. Information is becoming automatic – the student can more independently access the information. Teachers often become uncomfortable if a student is taking too long to respond; therefore, prompts and hints are often given to elicit a quicker response. The goal of this step is for the student to provide a response without teacher prompting within 0 - 2 seconds. Fluency is essential.

> *At the recall level, Jose can quickly name the emotions when he sees a facial expression. He can list a variety of reasons why someone would use a fake smile including the person feeling frustrated, arrogant, sad, or upset. Recall is often based on rote memory, and since rote memory skills are often a strength of the ASD neurology, many students excel during this stage.*

Application

At the application stage, the student applies the newly learned information in a controlled, yet meaningful or simulated real-life situation – often in the presence of a mentor. Examples include role-play sessions in the classroom to practice before an event and interactions in actual settings with the help of a coach, mentor, or teacher. At this level, the student is given the opportunity use the skill in a different context than what was originally learned.

Vermeulen (2012) has focused on the importance of context for learning, proposing that in order for individuals with HF-ASD to attain application-level skills, the concept of "context" must be integrated into application activities. As a result, if a learner is working on making comments in response to someone else's statement, several contexts must be considered. For example, what does "making a comment" look like when the learner is with (a) a teacher in class, (b) a known peer at recess, (c) a same age stranger at a park, (d) a cashier at the mall, and so forth? Vermeulen further suggests that we formalize these experiences by developing specific goals and activities that address context.

> *Jose reached application on the emotions he was taught with his peers in band practice, including when peers were hiding their true emotion behind a fake smile.*

Generalization

At the generalization level, the learner independently uses skills in different environments and conditions in which the skill was first learned. This is another place where the ASD neurology can present challenges. When the student reaches the generalization stage, skills are used in more natural and functional settings and under more varied conditions.

> *At this stage, Jose understands emotions of family members at home, the ticket taker at his local cinema, and the cashier at the grocery store.*

Maintenance

The final level, maintenance, involves periodic checks to ensure that acquired skills are intact. For children and youth with HF-ASD, this stage is particularly important – an acquired but infrequently used skill may be forgotten unless it is practiced. To counteract this, the teacher ensures that students have ongoing opportunities to use the skill.

> *Jose's teacher periodically asks him how people they both know are feeling and how he can tell. This informal interaction allows his teacher to determine whether this skill is still a part of Jose's repertoire.*

Summary

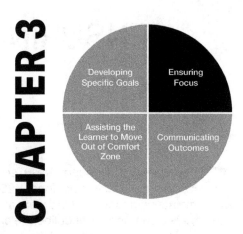

CHAPTER 3

Our goals can only be reached through a vehicle of a plan, in which we must fervently believe, and upon which we must vigorously act. There is no other route to success.

– Pablo Picasso

This adequately summarizes the importance of goal setting!

ENSURING FOCUS

When you feel in your gut what you are and then dynamically pursue it – don't back down and don't give up – then you're going to mystify a lot of folks. **– Bob Dylan**

Focus means to concentrate on something and pay particular attention to it (Merriam-Webster Dictionary, 2006). According to Ericsson and Pool, maintaining focus "is hard work and it is generally not fun" (p. 81). Nevertheless, it is a component of deliberate practice required to gain critical mass and, therefore, is indispensable. Without motivation, we will not be able to sustain the attention to practice skills until we reach critical mass. Thus, motivation, attention, and time are interrelated components of focus.

Motivation

Motivation, the general desire or willingness to engage in an activity or behavior, is necessary for learning because it …

- Directs behavior toward specific goals,
- Leads to increased effort and energy,
- Increases initiation of and persistence in activities,
- Determines which consequences are positive or negative,
- Enhances performance (Ormrod, 2008).

In other words, motivation is essential.

To do something – anything – we need motivation. Even simple acts such as talking, eating, and driving to the store require some degree of motivation (Deckers, 2015). Motivation is impacted by two major factors: (a) whether we think we are likely to be successful and (b) the value we place on achieving the goals (Huitt, 2011; Locke et al., 1981; Vroom, 1964). Within education, research shows that motivation occurs when there are positive teacher-student relationships, positive peer attention, and when student's special interests are incorporated into tasks. Finally, motivation is encouraged when students know that some sort of reinforcement system is in place and is available to them. Each of these areas is discussed below.

Perceived Probability of Success

Often individuals with HF-ASD are thought to be unmotivated, even if unintentionally. This is understandable when we consider how often the learner has experienced failure. These failures often trigger memories of past anxieties and can cause avoidance and self-preservation responses. Repeated failure can create a sense of futility and frustration.

Learners who experience frequent failure often develop *learned helplessness*, whereby they do not attempt a task because they know they are destined to fail. Thus, a lack of motivation may be related to a learner's lack of past success (cf. Stewart, 1996).

Success breeds success. If you structure activities so that the student experiences success, he will be more likely to engage in future activities because he is more confident. Further, it is essential to encourage learners by reminding them that they that they *can* learn a skill or accomplish a task. For students who are less confident about their abilities, it is important to validate their feelings and let them know that your role is to support them and lead them toward success.

The following are some statements that you can use to help individuals with ASD understand that they can be successful:

- "I'll help you get good at ..."
- "We'll just work on it until you get it."
- "I'll teach you how to ..."
- "We won't move on to the next step until you've mastered the first step."
- "Practicing will help you to be more comfortable."
- "This is something that will help you later in life."
- "Do you want to feel more comfortable with ...?"
- "You may have had bad experiences in the past. I'm here to help you to be more successful" (Mataya, Aspy, & Shaffer, 2017, p. 14).

If we are not able to link our success to our work, we may be less likely to engage with a task. On the other hand, the ability to see potential success may decrease learned helplessness and increase willingness to take on difficult tasks and new challenges. This results in students "buying in" or being invested in learning the task (cf. Wolfberg, Bottema-Beutel, & DeWitt, 2012).

> *Not knowing the cause of one's successes and failures undermines one's motivation to work on associated tasks.*
> – Jacquelynne S. Eccles & Allan Wigfield

True "buy-in" often does not occur until a student begins to experience success. If the student has a positive relationship and has experienced past success with you, this can be used as a way of facilitating buy-in for future events.

How do you help somebody with HF-ASD see this connection? In general, use logical reasoning because most individuals with ASD understand some form of logic. While using logic, you are teaching (a) reasoning, (b) how parts of a whole work together to produce an outcome, (c) problem solving, and (d) making judgments and decisions. To underscore the importance of all this, The Framework for 21st Century Learning (P21: Partnership for 21st Century Learning, n.d.) recognizes these as the skills and knowledge students need to succeed in work, life, and citizenship.

When teaching, be visual because the majority of individuals do their best learning when visual supports are used (Hellendoom, Langstraat, Wijn-roks, Buitelaar, van Daalen,& Leseman, 2014). T-charts, social narratives, mapping, video modeling, and cartooning are all helpful when working with learners on the spectrum. More information on these strategies can be found in the Appendix.

Value of Achieving the Goal

Learning why a skill is important may vary from student to student. In order to take the first step toward critical mass on any skill, the student must see some importance for the skill. The importance may be related to (a) how it will help the learner today, (b) how it will help the learner in the future, or (c) whether the learner will receive a reinforcer if he engages in an activity or completes a task. How a skill is presented affects students' motivation to learn it.

> Phrases like "because I said so" and "that makes your teacher feel disappointed" do not help students with ASD connect value to a goal that has been set.

Relationships With Teachers

In their seminal study on teacher-student relationships, Aspy and Roebuck (1977) found that five teacher behaviors were strongly related to students' social and academic gains: (a) accepts student feelings, (b) uses praise, (c) accepts and/or uses student ideas, (d) provides instruction and (e) justifies authority. The authors further reported that it is "... worthwhile making sure that teachers use high levels of interpersonal skills in interactions with their students because benefits accrue to the students in terms of increases on both mental health and cognitive indices" (p. 223).

More recent research, including a meta-analysis of over 350,000 students, supports the findings of Aspy and Roebuck (1977) and reveals that the quality of early teach-er-student relationships has a long-lasting impact (Cornelius-White, 2007). The studies analyzed by Cornelius-White identified additional supportive teacher behaviors as well as learner outcomes. These appear in Table 3.1.

Table 3.1
Teacher Relationships and Student/Classroom Outcomes

Teacher Behaviors That Indicate a Positive Relationship With Students	Student Outcomes
• Engages in little conflict • Is supportive of student needs • Is empathetic • Supports independent and interdependent functioning/not dependence • Is trustworthy • Is positive • Feels close to students • Accepts student ideas • Praises/reinforces • Accepts student feelings • Is sensitive to individual differences • Involves students in decision-making • Is warm • Is respectful • Encourages high-level thinking • Is responsive to learner developmental, social, and personal needs • Promotes student success • Is genuine	• Has better social skills • Accepts peers • Develops social connections • Follows rules • Has higher academic performance • Is academically resilient • Attends school regularly, lower absenteeism • Is self-directed • Participates in class • Rates self as satisfied with school • Is less likely to drop out • Is cooperative • Has better mental health • Explores options for higher education • Has good self-esteem/self-concept • Adjusts better to school academically and socially • Is academically engaged • Is motivated • Is less likely to be lonely • Likes school • Shows self-control • Exhibits less defiant behavior/aggression

Adapted from Cornelius-White, J. (2007). Learner-centered teacher-student relationships are effective: A meta-analysis. *Review of Educational Research, 77*(1), 113-143.

Ongoing positive teacher-student relationships in elementary school increase the likelihood that the learner will experience fewer episodes of negative behavior. In addition, students who have a positive relationship with teachers in kindergarten also have higher academic achievement, fewer behavioral problems, and better social skills through the eighth grade (cf. McCormick & O'Connor, 2015; O'Connor, Collins, & Supplee, 2012) and into high school (Murray & Malmgren, 2005). This clearly impacts the long-term trajectory of school and, eventually, employment (Baker, Grant, & Morlock, 2008; O'Connor et al., 2012).

Teachers who are in negative relationships with learners tend to feel frustrated, irritable, and angry. They often engage in educational bullying. Educational bullying occurs when adults who are members of the school staff use their power intentionally or unintentionally to cause students distress. Educators who bully tend to yell, make snide or sarcastic comments, and use harsh punitive control to manage behavior (Heinrichs, 2005). These teachers often describe themselves as "struggling" or "in constant conflict" and describe students as "exhausting" or "leaving them feeling drained and burned out" (Rimm-Kaufman et al., 2002). Students in the classroom of such teachers not only fail to reap the benefits of academic and social improvement, they are also rejected, victimized, and bullied by classmates who model the inappropriate teacher behavior (Gallagher, 2013).

How important are teacher-student relationships for learners on the spectrum? VERY! Teachers set the stage for student social success. *Students with ASD who have a positive relationship with their teachers have a higher level of social inclusion, have more peer relationships, and experience fewer behavior problems* (Robertson, Chamberlain, & Kasari, 2003).

Thus, it is essential that a teacher mentor have a strong relationship with the student. Overall, mentors ensure that students know the path to excellence and understand that they can learn new skills. In order for this to occur, mentors must:
- Be trained.
- Support the student to learn skills that others learn implicitly (i.e., social skills, daily living skills).
- Be available on a daily basis.

Use their positive relationship with the student to set goals, encourage focus, provide ongoing information about the learner's outcome, and push the student past her comfort zone.

Positive Peer Attention

Most individuals with ASD want friends but may not have the necessary skills to establish and maintain friendships. Peer helpers, Circle of Friends, lunch buddies, and opportunities for supported friendships can all be motivators for the individual with ASD (Schlieder, 2007). Involving NT peers as facilitators for individuals with ASD is collectively known as a peer-mediated intervention (cf. Chan, Lang, Rispoli, O'Reilly, Sigafoos & Cole, 2009) – an EBP (CMS, 2010; NAC, 2009, 2015; NPDC, 2009, 2015).

Peer-mediated interventions, which incorporate myriad instructional strategies, occur when trained neurotypical (NT) peers teach or support the use of academic or social skills for learners with special needs, including those with ASD. Some students with HF-ASD benefit from being in a peer group with those who are working on similar challenges when a good peer match is made with reciprocal language abilities. For many students with HF-ASD, a group that contains NT peers can be daunting due to the large difference in social abilities across the two groups.

The importance of providing students with HF-ASD opportunities to develop relationships cannot be overestimated. For example, the National Technical Assistance Center on Transition (NTACT; n.d.) has identified a collaborative network of student support as one the predictors of adult success for individuals with special needs.

Special Interests

A lack of motivation may result from *our* failure to understand what motivates the learner on the spectrum (Koegel & Mentis, 1985; Calder, Hill, & Pellicano, 2013). Quite often it is not necessary to look beyond the student's special interest to identify the best motivator (Winter-Messiers et al., 2007).

> Between 75% (Klin, Danovitch, Merz, & Volkmar, 2007) and 90% (Bashe & Kirby, 2010) of individuals on the spectrum develop deep and intense interests compared to 30% of their NT peers.

When interviewed about their special interests, children and adults with HF-ASD reported that they felt a greater sense of confidence and positivity when engaged with their areas of special interest (Winter-Messiers et al., 2007).

Building learning activities around the individual's interests helps to provide motivation to learn new knowledge and skills. Further, incorporating special interest interventions, such as the Power Card Strategy (Gagnon & Myles, 2016), can increase motivation as well as skill acquisition (for resources on the Power Card Strategy, refer to the Appendix. Winter-Messiers (2007) describes the impact of integrating special interests into instruction (see Figure 3.1).

Academics	• High motivation and increased focus • Higher Quality of work
Communication	• Focused conversation • Advanced vocabulary • More appropriate body language
Social	• More willing to interact • More able to discern social cues and develop social strategies
Emotional	• Lower anxiety and more relaxed • Fewer meltdowns
Sensory	• Improved sensory processing • Higher tolerance of sensory violations
Executive Function	• Improved focus and memory • Better planning and organization skills

Figure 3.1. The impact of integrating special interests into academic tasks for the learner with ASD.

Adapted from M. A. Winter-Messiers (2007). Toilet brushes and tarantulas: Understanding the origin and development of special interest areas in children and youth with Asperger's syndrome. *Journal of Remedial and Special Education, 28(3), 140-152.*

Opportunities to Earn Reinforcers

It is not uncommon to think about motivation as an internal characteristic while acknowledging that behavior can also be influenced by external factors. For many, including those on the spectrum, external reinforcers are necessary for learning to occur. This is supported by neurological research (Kohls et al., 2012; Zeeland et al., 2010).

As a result, opportunities to earn reinforcers can be extremely motivating for all learners, including those with ASD. For example, first/then schedules visually pair an activity with its reinforcer. Knowing that reinforcers will be available when meeting criteria on point sheets, contracts, self-monitoring sheets, and the Travel Card (Carpenter, 2005) can also be motivating (see Appendix).

> For some individuals with ASD, reinforcement is a contentious topic. The word "reinforcement" itself sparks anger. These advocates hold that reinforcement has been utilized in an attempt to eliminate neurodiversity or to prevent people with ASD from being who they are. That is an important perspective. It is also true that all learners benefit from the use of reinforcement as they move toward critical mass. There is no way to get there without it. It is possible and necessary to both embrace the role of reinforcement and the value of neurodiversity.

Adults can inadvertently reinforce negative behavior using reinforcers. Teachers should be knowledgeable about what behavior of the student is being reinforced. For example, a child can begin yelling out in class and the teacher may offer a "bribe," such as "be quiet until the lesson is over and you will earn computer time" – to keep peace in the classroom. Although this makes it easier for the short-term, it makes the behavior more difficult for the long-run.

Attention

*Attention is the holy grail. Everything that you
are conscious of, everything you let in,
everything you remember and forget, depends on it.*
— David Strayer (cited in Richtel)

Many learners with ASD have challenges related to the ability to attend. In fact, approximately 60% of learners on the spectrum receive an attention-deficit hyperactivity disorder (ADHD) diagnosis before being diagnosed with ASD (Harvey, Lugo-Candelas, & Breaux, 2015; Jónsdóttir, Saemundsen, Antonsdóttir, Sigurdardóttir, & Ólason, 2011). Even those on the spectrum who do not have this diagnosis often exhibit attention challenges (Harvey et al., 2015).

> An initial diagnosis of ADHD can delay an ASD diagnosis for up to three years (Miodovnik, Harstad, Sideridis, & Huntington, 2015).

So how do we increase the attention of individuals with ASD? Ways to increase attention include (a) structured background activities (b) priming, (d) predictability and placement in the environment, (d) minimizing distractions (unless you are trying to teach how to handle distractions), (e) signaling, and (f) exercise or movement. Each of these will be described in the following.

Structured Background Activities

Sometimes people, both with and without ASD, are better able to learn when they engage in a "background" activity that does not place a cognitive demand. For example, some students can concentrate better on a lecture when they are allowed to engage in an activity, such as drawing or doodling. Chewing gum, drinking water, pacing, moving on a disco seat, listening to classical music, and manipulating a fidget are other simple background activities that may enhance concentration. A list of sample background activities appears in Table 3.2.

Table 3.2
Background Activities That Can Enhance Neural Noise and Impact Learning

Inflatable disc	Velcro™, scratchy side up, under desktop
Disc 'O' Sit™	Coffee stirrers
Camping pillow	Brushing hair
Therapy putty	Latex-free tubing
Playdoh™	Straws
Koosh Ball	Weighted lap buddy
Tangle™	Not requiring direct eye contact
Fidgets	Sturdy straw to drink from
Drawing	Gummy worms (chill to harden)
Hand lotion	Crunchy or chewy snacks
Chewing gum	Rocking in a rocking chair
Jujubes	Tennis ball on diagonal legs of chair
Weighted vest	
Hard candy	Allow individual to stand or walk
Rubberized shelf-lining on chair seat	

Many background activities are sensory-based. We use them, both consciously and subconsciously, to adjust our focus and attention on a daily basis (Leekam, Neito, Libby, Wing, & Gould, 2007; Myles, Mahler & Robbins, 2014). For example, when you are sitting in a meeting and feel your attention level drop, you might notice changes in your body (e.g., your eyes are droopy, your brain is fuzzy/sleepy, your body is heavy). But this is an important meeting, and you know your boss, who is sitting across the table, is watching you. You realize that sipping cold water, chewing on a mint, and shaking your leg up and down under the table are helpful. All of these sensory activities begin to increase your attention. You start to feel more alert and focused.

Research in neuroscience, psychology, biology, medicine, and meteorology is beginning to shed light on how these background or noncognitive activities – scientifically referred to as "noise" or "neural noise" – enhance learning and functioning. (In this case, "noise" does not refer to sound; rather, it refers to minor, nonstimulating, background activities that provide focus rather than distraction [Levin & Miller, 1996; Moss, Ward & Sannita, 2004; Simmons & Milne, 2014].) For example, studies have found that individuals with ASD have less neural noise than typically developing people (Davis & Plaisted-Grant, 2014) and, thus, may need pre-planned background activities.

It is key that the background activity is planned in advance so that it is not distracting to the individual or class; otherwise, it can stop learning from occurring or slow it down. Likewise, it is essential that selected background activities do not require concentration so that the learner can focus on the task at hand.

How can you determine whether a background activity is needed? Observe the individual with ASD in learning situations. When he is engaged in effective learning, what does he do?

- Manipulate an object, such as hair twirling, playing with a fidget, biting nails, drawing, taking apart a pen?
- Engage in body movements, such as rocking back and forth, tapping feet, flapping?

In addition, you may introduce some background activities and take data on skill acquisition to determine whether the learner needs this type of support. Consultation with an occupational therapist or autism specialist to identify potential background activities may also be helpful.

Do all individuals with ASD need "neural noise" to attend? Of course, not. But for those who have difficulties attending without a background activity, incorporating one into the student's instruction can support skill acquisition, thereby enhancing the ability to achieve critical mass.

Priming

Priming introduces information or activities prior to their use or occurrence (Wilde, Koegel, & Koegel, 1992). The purposes of this intervention are to (a) familiarize the student with the material before its actual use; (b) introduce predictability into the information or activity, thereby reducing stress and anxiety; and (c) increase successful performance.

Priming is an antecedent-based intervention – an EBP.

In priming, the actual materials that will be used in a lesson are shown to the student the day, the evening, or even as late as the morning before the activity is to take place, and the student is reinforced for attending to the materials. In some cases, priming occurs right before the activity, such as when a peer mentor overviews what will take place during the science experiment immediately prior to the beginning of science class. Priming is not limited to academics. It can include an introduction to a new environment (i.e., what does the stage look like for the assembly) or a new material (i.e., touching finger paint before art class). It can occur either in the classroom or at home. It can be done by a parent at home or by a paraprofessional, a resource teacher, or a trusted peer at school (Myles & Aspy, 2016).

Although Wilde and colleagues (1992) recommend that the actual teaching materials, such as a worksheet or textbook, be used in priming, in some cases, priming has been successful using a list or a description of the activities that take place along with the student's daily schedule.

Priming is most effective when it is built into the student's routine. It is important to keep in mind that priming is *not* teaching, correcting, or testing.

Priming is merely an introduction to what will happen during an activity (cf. Crosland & Dunlap, 2012). To be effective, it should occur in an environment that is relaxing and given by a person who is patient and encouraging. Finally, priming sessions should be short, providing a brief overview of the academic and/or behavior expectations in each class.

Predictability and Placement in the Environment

Clinical reports reveal that individuals with ASD have meltdowns as a response to change or engage in restricted interests and repetitive behaviors in order to prevent or minimize change because the autism neurology reacts negatively to a lack of predictability (Gomot & Wicker, 2012). In fact, individuals with ASD process a small change, such as being picked up by their parent 5 minutes before an event ends rather than right on time, in the same way NT individuals process a major change, such as losing their job. This can explain why a meltdown occurs when a child with ASD is told to wear a nonpreferred shirt without advance warning.

It is not surprising that the crucial need to maintain sameness can interfere with learning and functioning in a highly unpredictable world. So, in order to maximize learning, the environment must be predictable, and this predictability must be communicated to the student in a manner that is compatible with her learning style to help to reduce fear of the unknown.

> *"I remember processing every small change as a life-changing event. It was exhausting. I could not focus. I could not learn. I demanded predictability with words and behavior. Now I have learned how to create predictability for myself and to tolerate a lack of predictability. It has been a journey!"* Simone, age 27

One way to establish predictability is to set up routines. Routines are important in everybody's life. Whether morning routines, bedtime routines, or workplace routines, routines provide comfort and ease.

When establishing routines for students with HF-ASD, be careful not to make the student overly rigid. For example, while doing the same thing every day may make the learner more comfortable, it will also make him more rigid. So, build in changes periodically to help the student to be more flexible. Support changes by using priming and a visual schedule that highlights schedule changes. In addition, having the student practice daily events can be effective. For some learners, it is helpful to teach the routine and then gradually add variety to shape their tolerance for change.

Student placement in the classroom should also be considered. A consistent place in the room increases predictability. Thus, when assigning seat-ing to students with HF-ASD, make sure the student is placed such that the teacher can easily monitor the student's attention to task without calling undue notice to this precautionary measure.

In addition, Sona Chadwick (personal communication, 2000) recommends placing carefully selected nondisabled peers at least two deep in all directions from the student with ASD. These students can cue the child with ASD to attend or to turn to the right page in the book or assignment. This configuration can also help prevent bullying.

Finally, it is important that learners understand their environment and the elements within it. For students with HF-ASD, this often requires direct instruction. Collateral advantages of a predictable environment with careful classroom placement include decreased anxiety and a limited need to focus on the environment so that the student can pay more attention to the task at hand.

Minimizing Distractions

The physical environment should be carefully arranged to minimize distractions that are often sensory-based. Possible strategies include not placing a child near a window or loud heater vent, allowing a visually sensitive learner to wear a baseball cap in class, unscrewing a fluorescent bulb and using an incandescent lamp instead, or a combination of these suggestions. Avoiding placement in high-traffic areas (e.g., near the waste basket, pencil sharpener, or door) also minimizes distraction. An occupational therapist or autism specialist can be helpful in identifying and implementing these types of supports.

It is important to look beyond the physical environment when addressing distractions. Learners with HF-ASD experience internal distractions, such as the second grader who is not able to focus on math if he is still thinking about a problem with a peer on the playground. Or the teenage boy who is not able to concentrate in language arts if he is sitting behind a girl he has a crush on.

Distractions can be based in the present or the past. It is not uncommon for a learner with ASD to dwell on an event that happened weeks or years ago and have difficulty resolving the issues well enough to focus.

> Seventeen-year-old Maria became distressed when told to work with Sam, a classmate, because he had not invited her to his third-grade birthday party and had yet to apologize.

These challenges must be addressed through a combination of EBPs, which may include visual supports, cartooning, social narratives, the Power

Card Strategy (Gagnon & Myles, 2016), and the Problem Solving Rubric (Mataya & Owens, 2013) (see the Appendix for additional information).

Signaling

Signaling occurs when the teacher discretely provides a cue to refocus the learner's attention (Long, Morse, & Newman, 1976). For example, when a student begins to exhibit off-task behavior, the teacher uses a nonverbal signal to help the student reorient. The teacher can place herself in a position where the student can see the teacher's face or use a "secret "signal between herself and the student as redirection. Some use such signals as tapping on the child's desk, clearing their throat, showing a visual, pointing toward the sentence that another student is reading, lightly touching the student on his shoulder, or motioning to the task.

Exercise or Movement

Regular physical exercise or movement is an EBP, which can reduce stress, increase attention, and help the individual to be ready to learn. Further, exercise has been shown to decrease repetitive behavior, aggression, off-task behavior and elopement. In addition, it has resulted in increases in on-task behavior, academic responding, and appropriate motor behavior (Lang et al., 2010).

For some, movement is helpful before an activity as it increases attention to task. For others, movement after the task releases stress, making them more ready for the next task. A physical education teacher or occupational therapist can help identify important variables regarding exercise and movement, such as ...

- What types of exercise or movement are appropriate?
- Should exercise or movement be provided on a scheduled basis?
- Should exercise or movement be provided on an as-needed basis?
- How long and with what intensity should exercise or movement be provided?
- How should impact of exercise or movement be measured?
- Should reinforcement (see page 50) be incorporated into exercise or movement?

> Understanding the 8th sensory system, interoception, is prerequisite to knowing when exercise or movement can be helpful. Interoception helps us feel sensations inside our body, including pain, body temperature, itch, sexual arousal, hunger, thirst, heart rate, breathing rates, muscle

---

2   The term *intense practice* does not refer to rote practice. It refers to practice at all levels of learning: awareness, recognition, recall, application, generalization, and maintenance.

tension, sleepiness and when we need to use the bathroom. Interoception can be at the root of an individual not feeling or recognizing that he is stressed or not understanding that he has exercised to the point he is sick or overly fatigued. Information on this often neglected system may be found in *Interoception: The 8th Sensory System* by Kelly Mahler.

This intervention may include walking to school in the morning, jogging around a track, swimming, or walking the track before a pep rally or other activity that is stressful to the student.

Put in the Time

As a rule of thumb, I think that anyone who hopes to improve skill in a particular area should devote an hour or more each day to practice that can be done with full concentration.
– Anders Ericsson & Robert Pool

Everyone must put in the time to learn.

Several researchers (e.g., Bloom, 1985; Ericsson, Krampe, & Tesch-Römer, 1993) encourage teachers to schedule regular, deliberate practice periods of a relatively fixed duration for all learners. At first, intensive practice[2] may be limited to 10-20 minutes per session. As learners become comfortable with the brief sessions, the level of practice is increased. Ericsson and Pool (2017) recommend that the goal should be at least one hour per day of deliberate practice. Not everyone agrees that one hour per day is the magic number; however, researchers and practitioners alike support the use of frequent, intense sessions that match the needs of learners. This applies not only to learning social, communication, and daily living skills, but also to gymnastics, internal medicine, and music (cf. Ericsson, 2006, 2008; Wayne et al., 2006).

In reality, putting in the time cannot be separate from motivation and attention. According to Ericsson and Pool (2017), it is better to learn and practice skills with 100% effort for less time than at 70% effort for a longer period. They further recommend that once a learner can no longer focus effectively, it is time to end the session.

It is particularly important that individuals on the spectrum have the opportunity to "put in the time." The ASD neurology places challenges on implicit learning. Thus, skills that others learn implicitly – social, communication, and daily living skills – must be taught during regularly scheduled intensive practice sessions. While academic skills may be taught through lectures and demonstration, social skills instruction must include practice and performance (Bellini, 2016). Unless this happens, the current dismal outcomes in employment, independent living, and community participation will not improve.

Supporting the work of Ericsson (2006, 2008) and Bellini (2016), in a study on the effectiveness of social skills programs, Bellini, Peters, Benner, and Hopf (2007) concluded that schools should increase the intensity of social skills instruction. They stated, "School personnel should look for opportunities to teach and reinforce social skills as frequently as possible throughout the school day" (p. 160). This also applies to communication and daily living skills.

Summary

Currently, the school, as a system, overwhelmingly supports instruction in academic areas for learners with HF-ASD. It does not appear to place a high value on the impact of having good social, communication, and daily living skills. Thus, it is incumbent on us to "put in the time" for instruction and practice in these areas to enhance the quality of life for individuals with HF-ASD. And to ensure adequate focus, we must attend to learner motivation and attention.

COMMUNICATING OUTCOMES

Generally speaking, no matter what you're trying to do, you need feedback to identify exactly where and how you are falling short. Without feedback — either from yourself or from outside observer — you cannot figure out what you need to improve on or how close you are to achieving your goals.

– Ericsson & Pool

In the social world, feedback or information about the learner's outcomes is almost constant. It may be direct – "good idea," "no thank you" – or subtle – a sideways glance or "we'll see." For individuals on the spectrum, this type of information that would be clear to most people may be confusing or undetected. Worse yet, when information about outcomes is eventually given, it is often communicated in a negative and discouraging manner.

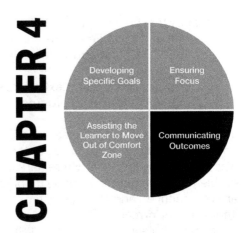

CHAPTER 4

Developing Specific Goals

Ensuring Focus

Assisting the Learner to Move Out of Comfort Zone

Communicating Outcomes

Judy Endow, a woman on the spectrum, describes the typical manner in which she hears about the outcomes of "social sins", such as "everybody knows …," "common sense tells you …," "it is quite obvious that …," or "I shouldn't have to tell you, but …" She also talks about the cumulative impact of these experiences.,

> As an adult with autism, I have learned that whenever somebody says one of these phrases what is coming next is an explanation of some sort of social sin I have committed. Not understanding … contributes to the often pervasive feeling that goes far beyond not fitting in, to feeling that you are not part of the human race. During my growing-up years, I believed for a long time that I was an alien (Endow, 2006, personal communication).

Such experiences contribute to social isolation. The individual knows that *something* is "wrong" and may begin to believe that *she*, instead of a specific act or behavior, is "wrong" but has no idea of how to fix it. What results are (a) avoidance of environments in which unclear information is given, (b) reduced self-confidence, and/or (c) potential depression or anxiety – all of which may stop future learning from occurring.

The communicating outcomes step of *deliberate practice* provides a way to change this pervasive pattern.

Providing Immediate and Informative Feedback and Evaluation

We all need people who will give us feedback. That's how we improve.
– Bill Gates

According to Wiggins (2012), "Decades of education research support the idea that by teaching *less* and providing *more* feedback, we can produce greater learning" (p. 2). Feedback and evaluation provide information about how we are doing in our efforts to achieve a goal.

> Evaluation in this context refers to informal and formal means of measuring progress.

In deliberate practice, progress is monitored and feedback and evaluation are carefully designed. The student is given specific information on what he is doing right and where things are going wrong. By identifying problems, future practice can be modified to correct errors. When errors are not identified and eliminated, time spent in practice does not result in improved performance. Feedback is the most powerful single influence enhancing achievement (Hattie, 2008).

The following is important when providing feedback and evaluation to an individual with HF-ASD:

1. **Reference the goal.** Feedback should be connected to one specific goal or target that has been task analyzed or broken in small steps. The goal cannot be so general that it is confusing for the learner. For example, teachers often think that back and forth conversation is a specific goal. Unfortunately, this does not tell the learner what he should be doing in conversation whether it's asking questions, telling stories, or making comments. Even questions can be broken down into at least three types of questions, including questions to start a conversation, follow-up questions about what someone just said, or reciprocal questions.

2. **Provide actionable information.** Specificity is key to actionable feedback and evaluation. Whenever possible, feedback and evaluation should be data-based so that the learner has a benchmark for her performance. For example, she should know that she made three on-topic and two off-topic comments during today's practice conversation compared to Tuesday's practice conversation where she made one comment on-topic and five off-topic. Further, after feedback and evaluation are provided to the learner, she should understand exactly what she should do. She should not have to draw inferences about the next step. Actionable feedback may include a statement such as, "Next time, try ..."

3. **Be sensitive to the needs of the individual.** Most people respond positively to feedback and evaluation when delivered in a manner that is consistent with their learning style. For some, feedback and evaluation should be written or drawn out; others prefer verbal feedback with a written follow-up. In addition, most learners with

HF-ASD place high value on consistency and may be better able to process information when it is structured. For example, Mrs. Johnson always begins feedback and evaluation for her student, Booker, with the phrase, "Let's talk about ..." If the student embarrasses easily, feedback should be provided privately.

4. **Be timely.** Feedback should be provided as near in time to the event as possible. During application-oriented practice opportunities (see Table 4.1), it is often ideal to provide feedback and evaluation when a skill is used or should be used. In authentic situations, feedback and evaluation are best provided immediately following the event.

5. **Provide ongoing feedback.** In order to reach critical mass, individuals with HF-ASD require multiple feedback and evaluation sessions. Feedback and evaluation should occur whenever the learner engages in an application-oriented skill and whenever the learner is under supervision in an authentic situation. Students should be taught that feedback and evaluation are a part of the learning process.

6. **Talk both about the positives and the challenges.** It is important to address both what was done correctly and the specific changes that are needed. Learners should be taught that everyone has challenges and everyone can learn from their challenges – and that challenges are not inherently bad but merely a signal that instruction and support are needed. Consider using the structure of compliment, correct, compliment. That is, provide reinforcement frequently – more frequently than correction or redirection. Finally, feedback and evaluation should be genuine and kind.

7. **Reinforce each increment.** Learners should not have to wait for reinforcement until they have mastered an entire sequence of tasks. Rather they should be rewarded or reinforced for smaller behaviors that lead to the mastery of a task. The following section provides more information on reinforcement.

8. **Provide time for reflection.** It is often helpful to provide learners with time to think about the feedback and evaluation they have been given. Reflection may be encouraged by providing written information, including reflection questions, such as, "How did I do during ...?" "What did I do well?" "What will I try to do next time?" Why is this important to me? Reflection can occur through illustration, a sharing of information between learner and adult, or self-analysis. If an individual has problems with penmanship, reflection activities should not have a written component.

Table 4.1 provides an example of these feedback and evaluation elements used in an application-oriented session of students practicing how to ask questions during conversations.

Table 4.1
Feedback and Evaluation Used in Teaching Conversation Skills from "Talk with Me: A Step-By-Step Conversation Framework for Teaching Conversational Balance and Fluency."

Conversation Example With Prompts

The following example shows how prompts are used within a natural conversation. Throughout our sessions, we use a combination of verbal and visual prompts. The prompts are used to guide, redirect, refocus, and encourage students.

Age: 8 - 9 years old (3rd- 4th grade)

Gender: Male

Group Size: 2 students

Conversational Goals

Peer 1 – Step 2: Asking Questions

Peer 2 – Step 2: Asking Questions

Strategy for Teaching the Conversation Framework

Natural Conversation

Students' Conversation	Adult Prompts
	Mrs. Kerry: I said, "I saw that someone had on a Kasey Kahne hat and he said he was just at a NASCAR race." Follow-up question.
Peer 1: I like Kasey Kahne.	
	Mrs. Kerry: So that would be a comment. What can you ask *me* about what I just said? A follow-up question.
Peer 1 & 2: *Pause*	
(Peer 1 raising his hand)	Mrs. Kerry: I said, "I saw that someone had on a Kasey Kahne hat and he said he was just at a NASCAR race." You'd say, "Hey, Mrs. Kerry." Okay put your hand down so I can hear you.
Peer 1: What's going on?	
	Mrs. Kerry: What's going on? What does that have to do with NASCAR? If you said, "Are you watching NASCAR *today*," that would have to do with NASCAR. But what's going on doesn't have anything to do with NASCAR unless you connect "what's going on" *with* "NASCAR."
Peer 1 & 2: *Pause*	
	Mrs. Kerry: Guys, I want you to ask *me* a question about NASCAR, so you'd say, "Mrs. Kerry, have you seen NASCAR?"
Peer 2: Mrs. Kerry, have you seen NASCAR?	
	Mrs. Kerry: I haven't, but my brother loves NASCAR.
Peer 2: I used to love cars a lot. I used to collect them.	
	Mrs. Kerry: What's your follow-up question for me?
Peer 2: Do you like NASCAR?	
	Mrs. Kerry: Good; that is a follow-up question about me. It's important to be able to ask questions about other people. I have a follow-up question for you on the topic of NASCAR. Have you seen a NASCAR race?

From Mataya, K., Aspy, R., & Shaffer, H. (2017). *Talk with me: A step-by-step conversation framework for teaching conversational balance and fluency* (p. 44).

Using Reinforcement

"How do you keep going? That is perhaps the biggest question that anyone engaged in purposeful or deliberate practice will eventually face."
– Ericsson & Pool

Reinforcement is a form of feedback and evaluation that results in an increase in a behavior. In other words, it is reinforcement that keeps a learner moving forward.

A large body of research on the value of reinforcement has revealed that it is not possible for learning to occur without reinforcement (Aspy & Grossman, 2011; Baer, Wolf, & Risley, 1968; Cooper, Heron, & Heward, 2007). Reinforcement is more than just a reward; it is a powerful tool for teaching and maintaining desirable academic, communication, social, regulation, and daily living skills (Henry & Myles, 2013). Reinforcement reassures the individual that he is doing well (Wilhelm, 2009). According to Aspy and Grossman (2011), without reinforcement there is no intervention.

> Students with ASD may lack skills that their age mates have acquired. Therefore, they require instruction and reinforcement for specific behaviors that are generally assumed to have been mastered by those in their age group. This mistaken assumption may lead to punitive approaches to addressing failure to display a skill that has, in fact, never been taught or acquired (Aspy & Grossman, 2011).

Not only does reinforcement increase the likelihood that a behavior will occur, it also lets learners know when they have met expectations. Sometimes an individual on the spectrum engages in an expected behavior without realizing its importance. Without reinforcement, she is not likely to engage in that behavior again.

A reinforcer may be positive (giving a reward) or negative (taking away or reducing something aversive). The reinforcer can also be social or tangible. Finally, reinforcement may be part of a system that is used for the entire class. Regardless of type, it must be something the student is willing to work for. Everyone has reinforcer preferences, and these preferences differ from individual to individual. If a student has a special interest that is a good place to start.

> Students learn to raise their hand because they want to be called on. Children learn that when they complete their chores, they earn their allowance. Adults go to work because they want a paycheck. Further, provided that the consequence is desirable, the behavior will be displayed more often in the future. Individuals most often make choices that result in the greatest payoff (Aspy & Grossman, 2011).

For many, the natural consequences of displaying a skill are sufficient to support its occurrence. However, that may not be as reinforcing for those on the spectrum. For example, the natural consequence of greeting others may be a nonverbal response (e.g., smile, wave). But the value of this may be missed by many with ASD because of (a) a slower processing time, (b) attending to something other than the verbal or nonverbal response, (c) lack of understanding of the meaning of the verbal or nonverbal response, and so forth.

This raises an additional point to consider. The underlying ASD character-istics – specifically, attention problems, narrow and unusual interests, and decreased interest in social praise – can make reinforcement more chal-lenging (Aspy & Grossman, 2011).

Sometimes avoidance of an activity carries a greater incentive than does participation. For example, a person who struggles with understanding social interactions may find browsing the Internet more rewarding than interacting with family members. A student who finds heat and noise aver-sive may be more motivated to leave his work incomplete to avoid recess and stay in the air-conditioned classroom for study hall. These examples highlight that there may be important differences in what individuals with ASD find reinforcing compared to their neurotypical (NT) peers (Aspy & Grossman, 2011).

When teaching new skills, a minimal delay between behavior and rein-forcement is central to learning. As a skill is mastered, reinforcement is still required, but at a different rate or level, to maintain the behavior.

> It is important to teach students to reinforce themselves for "work-ing hard" rather than being smart because students have control over how hard they work, but have limited control over their level of intelligence. In addition, combining goal setting with reinforcement can help learners acquire skills more quickly.

Aspy (2007) has identified a "disability" that plagues many adults who sup-port those on the spectrum. This debilitating condition essentially serves to "cancel out" the impact of instruction. She refers to it as "reinforcement stinginess disorder (RSD). Table 4.2 provides the criteria for RSD.

Table 4.2
Reinforcement Stinginess Disorder

(A) Qualitative impairment in reinforcement delivery behaviors, as manifested by at least two of the following:

1. Marked impairment in the use of praise and positive feedback in response to the demonstration of new skills.
2. Failure to reinforce behaviors that were prompted or modeled.
3. A lack of spontaneous seeking to encourage achievement of others (e.g., by a lack of giving or delivering a reinforcer following a goal behavior).
4. Delay in or total lack of the development of compassion for those who are reinforced by nontraditional reinforcers or who achieve skills at a rate different from their typically-developing peers.
5. In individuals with adequate speech, marked impairment in the ability to distinguish "fair" from "equal."
6. Stereotyped and repetitive use of ineffective strategies, such as delivering punishment to change behaviors related to a neurological disorder.
7. Lack of varied, spontaneous approaches to maintaining meaningful reinforcers for all learners.

(B) Onset post 21 years of age.

(C) The disturbance is not better accounted for by a lack of common sense or the belief that you can "punish the autism" out of someone.

Hopefully, you do not have RSD. If you do, it can be easily overcome by consciously including reinforcement throughout the day.

Summary

In games, we know who has won ...
You get the reinforcement for having played well.
– Michael A. Stockpole

In life, you do not know if you have won unless you receive information about outcomes. Feedback occurs after an action has been evaluated, and reinforcement is like the pot of gold at the end of the rainbow. If you do not provide feedback, evaluation, and reinforcement, in essence you are limiting the ability of a person with ASD. ASD. In essence, you are limiting the ability of the person with ASD to access social information and increase social understanding and the result is that she is isolated because she doesn't know if what she did was correct or incorrect. Without direct feedback, evaluation, and reinforcement, to borrow a phrase from Pink Floyd, we are putting a brick in the wall of isolation. And "just another brick in the wall" of isolation is exactly the opposite of what we want for individuals with ASD.

CHAPTER 5

Developing
Specific Goals

Ensuring
Focus

Assisting the
Learner to Move
Out of Comfort
Zone

Communicating
Outcomes

ASSISTING LEARNERS TO MOVE OUT OF THEIR COMFORT ZONE

Life begins at the end of your comfort zone. – Neale Donald Walsch

Change is uncomfortable and, therefore, requires extra energy. When we first learn a new skill, we typically default to what we know already because it is easier and less challenging than using the new skill. We will continue to do this – even if it is not effective or efficient – until we have been taught something else and have had a lot of practice in doing it.

All humans have an *equilibrium* state. This term, as used in science, refers to a situation that is not undergoing change. In science, this state can be measured and assessed, and it will not change unless forced to change. The field of thermodynamics and others describe this state as one of equilibrium, or balance. Without instruction and practice, the situation does not change.

A system will do its best to save energy. This is one of the laws of thermodynamics (Josiah Willard Gibbs, cited in Klein, 1990).

So why is a skill not generalizing? One reason is that it requires too much energy on the part of the learner. New situations have an element of unpredictability, which is often difficult for those on the spectrum to accept and deal with. Therefore, we must teach and support the fact that a lack of predictability is not bad and that there is always "an answer" or clarity to a situation.

> When teaching a new skill, it is important that the learner is ready to move out of his comfort zone. How do you ac-complish that? First, you make sure that he has the needed supports. Structure, modifications, reinforcement, visual supports, antecedent-based interventions that address sensory and regulation needs, and communication/social supports that are a part of the learner's education plan must be in place. A high level of support is often needed to assist the learner in moving outside of his comfort zone. This high level of structure will allow the student to focus on the task at hand.

Helping learners move out of their comfort zone can be facilitated by (a) matching the student's ability to the demands of the task, (b) matching the student's ability to group size, and (c) preventing meltdowns.

Match Ability to Demands

In order for critical mass to occur, the expectations must be reasonable. That is, each lesson or unit of instruction must be developed so that learner with ASD can succeed, either independently or with assistance. Remember – achieving critical mass, by its very nature, promotes competence.

Levels of Demands

Three levels of demand occur during instruction: easy demands, challeng-ing/emerging demands, and demands that are too demanding (Vygotsky, 1978).

Easy. Easy tasks are those that can be accomplished independently with-out modifications or supports. If tasks are too easy, they do not facilitate the learning of new information. They do have a role, however, as they can be used to build a positive self-concept, fluidity of performance, and inde-pendent work skills. It is important that learners understand why they are doing easy tasks; otherwise, this type of task can result in behavior chal-lenges related to boredom.

Emerging. These are activities that learners can complete with assistance or supports. Presenting tasks at this level is appropriate when trying to teach new concepts that build on known skills and when seeking to gener-alize across settings or individuals. This can also be referred to as connect-ing patterns and experiences (see page 22). This is often the level at which instruction is provided.

Too Demanding. Tasks that are too demanding are too difficult for the student, even with assistance or support. Students for whom tasks are too demanding might not have the prerequisite skills or even be aware that a concept or element exists. Tasks that are too difficult may result in emotional and behavioral problems – feelings of being overwhelmed, meltdowns, failure, disruption to self and others, increased isolation, peer rejection, and so on (Aspy & Grossman, 2011). For these reasons, it is rarely appropriate to present a task that is too difficult.

Achieving the Balance

When providing instruction – typically using emerging tasks – it essential that the demands of the task match the learner's abilities. The following three questions must be answered to ensure the appropriate level of task demand.

1. Are you asking the learner to complete a task or skill that is too hard?

2. Are you asking the learner to complete a task or skill that has not been taught?

3. Are you asking the learner to complete a task or skill without providing the necessary supports?

The goal of answering these questions is to provide balance between demands and ability (see Figure 5.1).

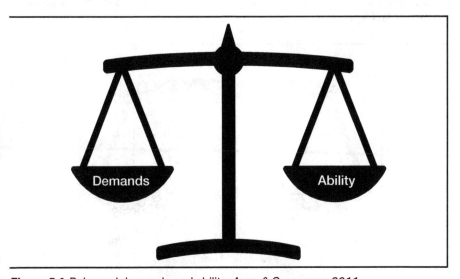

Figure 5.1. Balanced demands and ability. *Aspy & Grossman, 2011*

Figure 5.2 shows a case of imbalance between demands and ability for a group activity. The activity requires that the student listen, write, complete a task within a specific time limit, and interact with a group of five. Given this imbalance, the student is not likely to benefit from the activity.

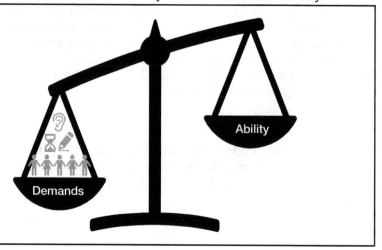

Figure 5.2. Demands exceed ability. *Aspy & Grossman, 2011*

How do you achieve balance? Balance may be obtained by decreasing or eliminating specific demands, providing supports, and/or teaching new skills. In doing so, it is important to conduct a task analysis to identify prerequisite and component skill deficits that need to be decreased or eliminated to teach and support new skills. Finally, skills to be taught should be prioritized, and the environment should be adapted to foster success, as illustrated in Figure 5.3 (see also Chapter IV).

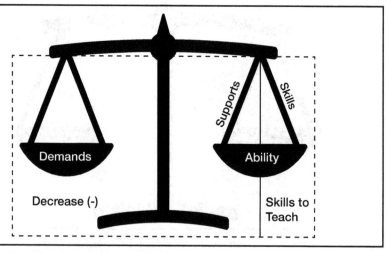

Figure 5.3. Methods to balance demands and ability: Provide support, teach skills, and decrease demands. *Aspy & Grossman, 2011*

Figure 5.4 shows one way to balance demands and activity for the group task introduced in Figure 5.2. As illustrated, the demand of writing was eliminated, group size was reduced, and supports were put in place to provide a balance, including a talking stick, a concrete support that the speaker holds when talking and a visual outline of the activity. The skill that the student was taught to enhance ability was conversational turn taking.

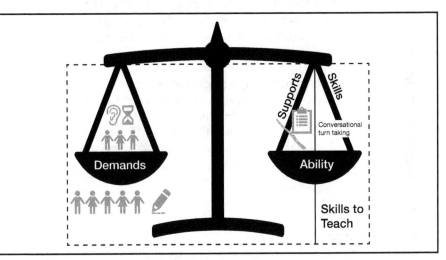

Figure 5.4. Balanced demands and abilities by providing support, teach skills, and decrease demands. *Aspy & Grossman, 2011*

Balance between demands and ability leads to successful acquisition of new skills – one step closer to achieving critical mass.

Match Ability to Group Size

Selecting the right learning environment for instruction is critical to learner success. Some students learn a new concept more easily individually or in a small group whereas others learn better in a whole-group setting. Most learners with ASD do best with a combination of these settings.

When the learner and group size is appropriately matched, the risk of a learner shutting down for feeling embarrassed because of not knowing an answer is decreased.

Easy tasks may be done in a whole group to increase confidence, especially if the student is learning to answer a question in front of the whole group. *Emerging tasks* may need instruction in an individual or small-group setting prior to exposure to the whole group so the learner gains confidence, thus increasing the likeliness that learning will occur. Participation in individual or small group classes (i.e., resource labs, academic enhancement) for pre- or reteaching opportunities can help the student on the spectrum better benefit from whole-group settings.

> Anthony, a 5-year-old student with ASD, was not familiar with many school-aged gym games, such as wall ball, four square, and red-light green-light. Most NT students learn these games in a gym or home setting with minimal instruction on the rules. But Anthony does not learn this way in a small group in gym. Rather than focusing on the rules of the new game – wall ball – he becomes anxious and begins hitting his peers.
>
> In order to match Anthony's ability to the group size, his teacher reduced the group size to 1:1 to teach the rules. After Anthony has learned the rules in this 1:1 setting, the teacher has him practice with one peer. The group size is increased to two peers, and so on, as he becomes successful.

Prevent Meltdowns

Approximately 80% of learners with ASD experience extreme anxiety (Salazar et al., 2015). This anxiety often develops into meltdowns as evidenced by the fact that 50% of individuals on the spectrum demonstrate this behavior.

Meltdowns are related to myriad issues, including (a) lack of predictability, (b) difficulty recognizing emotions in self and others, (c) challenges in matching emotions to events, and (d) problems remaining calm or calming self. The important thing for parents, teachers, and others to recognize and accept is that *meltdowns are not purposeful and are not planned in advance.*

> Missed clues from internal sensations, such as a fast heartbeat, may lead to meltdowns because the person with HF-ASD doesn't identify subtle feelings that signal the lead up to the meltdown. For more information, see *Interoception: The 8th Sensory System* by Kelly Mahler.

Further, it is important to understand that once somebody is experiencing heightened anxiety and/or embarks on the cycle of rage – rumbling rage, and recovery – he is not in a position to learn new information (Myles & Aspy, 2016). As shown in Figure 5.5, the only time that he can learn is when he is not experiencing heightened anxiety or the cycle of meltdowns. *As anxiety increases, the ability to learn decreases* (Wilhelm, 2009). Thus, it is important to have supports in place to ensure that the student is calm and ready to learn.

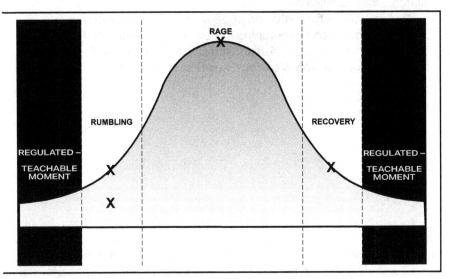

Figure 5.4. An individual with HF-ASD is ready to learn only when he is calm. From Myles, B. S., & Aspy, R. (2016). *High-functioning autism and difficult moments: Practical solutions for meltdowns.* Future Horizons. Used with permission.

> The concept of having mechanisms [in special education, we call mechanisms "antecedent-based interventions] in place to prevent meltdowns or explosions is used in biological, chemical, and mechanical systems; and in physics, human perception, and emotion (Knapen, Brascamp, Pearson, van Ee, & Blake, 2011; Wilhelm, 2009). For individuals with ASD, research has shown that meltdowns are neurologically based (Knapen et al., 2011) and are not purposeful and, thus, we must provide instruction as well as supports.

The needed supports differ by individual, setting, task demands, time of day, and many other variables. Systems, such as the comprehensive planning systems: the Ziggurat Model (Aspy & Grossman, 2011) and the Comprehensive Autism Planning System (CAPS; Henry & Myles, 2013), which are most often used together for individuals with ASD across the lifespan, can be invaluable in establishing a program that keeps a person calm and ready to learn. In addition, the SCERTS model (Social Communication/Educational Regulation/Transactional Support; Prizant, Wetherby, Rubin, Laurent, & Rydell, 2005) can be effective for preschool children.

A variety of EBPs may be embedded into the Ziggurat and CAPS models, including social narratives (Myles, 2005); the Incredible 5-Point Scale (Buron & Curtis, 2012), and priming (Wilde et al., 1992), all are antecedent-based interventions, and visual supports. EBPs are briefly discussed in Chapter VI (more information on this topic can be found at http://www. autisminternetmodules.org.

> Additional information on understanding and preventing meltdowns and intervening if they do happen can be found in *High-Functioning Autism and Difficult Moments: Practical Solutions for Meltdowns* by Brenda Smith Myles and Ruth Aspy.

Summary

When you go out of your comfort zone and it works, there is nothing more satisfying.

– Kristen Wiig

It is essential that we help individuals with ASD learn to embrace the need to move outside of their comfort zone because that is when real learning occurs and critical mass begins. When teachers respect the need for equilibrium while moving toward new achievements, we are helping learners gradually build new comfort zones and expand life options.

CHAPTER 6

Developing
Specific Goals

Ensuring
Focus

Assisting the
Learner to Move
Out of Comfort
Zone

Communicating
Outcomes

CHANGING OUTCOMES

When you have to make a choice and don't make it,
that in itself is a choice. **– William James**

We have a choice. If we are satisfied with current outcomes – individuals with ASD living with their parents throughout adulthood, being un- or under-employed, and having no friends – we can continue the course we're on.

In the United States, the law tells us that we must change course. That is, the Individuals With Disabilities Education Act (IDEA; 2004) states that the purpose of special education is to prepare students who have been identified with a disability for further education, employment, and independent living. Outcome data tells us that we are not meeting the requirements of this federal legislation.

The original standard for IDEA mandated educational benefits that were "merely more than *de minimis*." In other words, schools were responsible for providing education that leads to nontrivial benefits. While our students have made some progress in school across the years, this standard was not sufficiently challenging to result in positive outcomes for learners with special needs, including those with ASD. That is, students on the spectrum are not emerging from the public school system prepared for successful participation in further education, employment and independent living – perhaps due to previous acceptance of such low standards, especially in the areas of social, communication and daily living skills.

The new ruling in *Endrew F. v. Douglas County School District* (2016) requires schools "to offer an IEP reasonably calculated to enable a child to make progress appropriately ambitious in light of the child's circumstances." This means that an educational program must be designed to allow the child to progress from grade to grade as demonstrated by skill acquisition. Further, the school must provide a program that is "reasonably calculated to provide" the individual with educational opportunities that are "substantially equal" to those offered to other students.

Critical mass and the related science of deliberate practice will change the life course of individuals with ASD when these principles are applied to instruction in social, communication, and daily living skills. Incorporating the elements of deliberate practice – developing specific goals, ensuring focus, communicating outcomes, and assisting the learner to move out of the comfort zone – is a critical step toward helping individuals with ASD to reach their unlimited potential.

REFERENCES

Agran, M., Hughes, C., Thoma, C. A., & Scott, L. A. (2016). Employment social skills: What skills are really valued. *Career Development and Transition for Exceptional Individuals, 39*(2), 111-120.

Alderson-Day, B., & McGonigle-Chalmers, M. (2011). Is it a bird? Is it a plane? Category use in problem-solving in children with autism spectrum disorders. *Journal of Autism and Developmental Disorders, 41*(5), 555-565.

Aspy, D. M., & Roebuck, F. N. (1977). *Kids don't learn from people they don't like.* Amherst, MA: Human Resource Development Press.

Aspy, R. (2007, July). *Planning comprehensive behavior interventions for individuals with autism spectrum disorders.* Phoenix, AZ: Autism Society of America's 38th National Conference and Exposition on Autism Spectrum Disorder.

Aspy, R., & Grossman, B. G. (2011). *The Ziggurat Model: A framework for designing comprehensive interventions for individuals with high-functioning autism and Asperger syndrome.* Shawnee Mission, KS: AAPC Publishing.

Baer, D. M., Wolf, M. M., & Risley, T. R. (1968). Some current dimensions of applied behavior analysis. *Journal of Applied Behavior Analysis, 1*(1), 91-97.

Baker, J., Grant, S., & Morlock, L. (2008). The teacher-student relationship as a developmental context for children with internalizing or externalizing behavior problems. *School Psychology Quarterly, 23*(1), 3-15.

Bashe, P. R., & Kirby, B. L. (2010). *The OASIS guide to Asperger syndrome: Completely revised and updated: Advice, support, insight, and inspiration.* New York, NY: Crown Publishers.

Bellini, S. (2016). *Building social relationships: A systematic approach to teaching social interaction skills to children and adolescents with autism spectrum disorder and other social difficulties.* Shawnee Mission, KS: AAPC Publishing.

Bellini, S., Peters, J. K., Benner, L., & Hopf, A. (2007). A meta-analysis of school-based social skills interventions for children with autism spectrum disorders. *Remedial and Special Education, 28*(3), 153-162.

Bloom, B. S. (1985). Generalizations about talent development. In B. S. Bloom (Ed.), *Developing talent in young people* (pp. 507-549). New York, NY: Ballantine Books.

Blum, W. (2017). *The tipping point of success.* Retrieved from http://www.wendiblum.com/2012/02/the-tipping-point-of-success/.

Bock, M. A. (1994). Acquisition, maintenance, and generalization of a categorization strategy by children with autism. *Journal of Autism and*

Developmental Disorders, 24(1), 39-51.

Bock, M. A. (1999). Sorting laundry: Categorization strategy application to an authentic learning activity by children with autism. *Focus on Autism and Other Developmental Disabilities, 14*(4), 220-230.

Bock, M. A. (2001). SODA strategy: Enhancing the social interaction skills of youngsters with Asperger syndrome. *Intervention in School and Clinic, 36*(5), 272-278.

Bock, M. A. (2007). A social-behavioral learning strategy intervention for a child with Asperger syndrome. *Remedial and Special Education, 28*(5), 258-265.

Buron, K. D., & Curtis, M. (2012). *The Incredible 5-Point Scale: The significantly improved and expanded second edition; Assisting students in understanding social interactions and controlling their emotional responses.* Shawnee Mission, KS: AAPC Publishing.

Calder, L., Hill, V., & Pellicano, E. (2013). 'Sometimes I want to play by myself': Understanding what friendship means to children with autism in mainstream primary schools. *Autism, 17*(3), 296-316.

Carpenter, L. (2002). The travel card. In B. S. Myles & D. Adreon (Eds.), *Asperger Syndrome and adolescence: Practical solutions for school success* (pp. 92-96). Shawnee Mission, KS: AAPC Publishing.

Chan, J. M., Lang, R., Rispoli, M., O'Reilly, M., Sigafoos, J., & Cole, H. (2009). Use of peer-mediated interventions in the treatment of autism spectrum disorders: A systematic review. *Research in Autism Spectrum Disorders, 3*(4), 876-889.

Centers for Medicare and Medicaid Services. (2010). *Autism spectrum disorders: Final report on environmental scan.* Washington, DC: Author.

Cooper, J. O., Heron, T. E., & Heward, W. L. (2007). *Applied behavior analysis* (2nd ed.). Upper Saddle River, NJ: Pearson Education.

Cornelius-White, J. (2007). Learner-centered teacher-student relationships are effective: A meta-analysis. *Review of Educational Research, 77*(1), 113-143.

Crosland, K., & Dunlap, G. (2012). Effective strategies for the inclusion of children with autism in general education classrooms. *Behavior Modification, 36*(3), 251-269.

Davis, G., & Plaisted-Grant, K. (2014). Low endogenous neural noise. *Autism*, doi:10.1177/1362361314552198.

Deckers, L. (2015). *Motivation: Biological, psychological, and environmental.* East Sussex, UK: Psychology Press.

Endrew F. v Douglas County School District. *United States Court of Appeals for the Tenth Circuit.* (2016). Retrieved from https://www.supremecourt.gov/opinions/16pdf/15-827_0pm1.pdf.

Ericsson, K. A. (2006). The influence of experience and deliberate practice on the development of superior expert performance. *The Cambridge Handbook of Expertise and Expert Performance, 38*, 685-705.

Ericsson, K. A. (2008). Deliberate practice and acquisition of expert performance: a general overview. *Academic Emergency Medicine, 15*(11),

988-994.

Ericsson, K. A. (2016). Summing up hours of any type of practice versus identifying optimal practice hours: Commentary on Macnamara, Moreau, & Hambrick (2016). *Perspectives on Psychological Science, 11*(3), 351-354.

Ericsson, K. A., Krampe, R. T., & Tesch-Römer, C. (1993). The role of deliberate practice in the acquisition of expert performance. *Psychological Review, 100*(3), 363.

Ericsson, A., & Pool, R. (2017). *Peak: Secrets from the new science of expertise.* New York, NY: First Mariner Books.

Fazio, R. L., Pietz, C. A., & Denney, R. L. (2012). An estimate of the prevalence of autism spectrum disorders in an incarcerated population. *Journal of Forensic Psychology, 4,* 69-80.

Fiebelkorn, I. C., Foxe, J. J., McCourt, M. E., Dumas, K. N., & Molholm, S. (2013). Atypical category processing and hemispheric asymmetries in high-functioning children with autism: Revealed through high-density EEG mapping. Cortex, 49, 1259-1267.

Fields, C. (2012). Do autism spectrum disorders involve a generalized object categorization and identification dysfunction? *Medical Hypotheses, 79*(3), 344-351.

Gagnon, E., & Myles, B. S. (2016). *The Power Card Strategy 2.0: Using special interests to motivate children and youth with autism spectrum disorder.* Shawnee Mission, KS: AAPC Publishing.

Gallagher, E. (2013). *The effects of teacher-student relationships: Social and academic outcomes of low-income middle and high school students.* Retrieved from steinhardt,nyu.edu/opus/issues/2013/fall/gallagher.

Gastgeb, H. Z., Dundas, E. M., Minshew, N. J., & Strauss, M. S. (2012). Category formation in autism: Can individuals with autism form categories and prototypes of dot patterns? *Journal of Autism and Developmental Disorders, 42*(8), 1694-1704.

Ghoshal, A. (2016, May). Google's AI has read enough romance novels to write one on its own. *TNW.* Retrieved from https://thenextweb.com/google/2016/05/05/googles-ai-read-enough-romance-novels-write-one/#.

Gladwell, M. (2002). *The tipping point: How little things can make a big difference.* New York City, NY: Back Bay Books.

Gomot, M., & Wicker, B. (2012). A challenging, unpredictable world for people with autism spectrum disorder. *International Journal of Psychophysiology, 83*(2), 240-247.

Grandin, T. (1995). How people with autism think. In E. Schopler & G. B. Mesibov (Eds.), *Learning and cognition in autism* (pp. 137-156). New York, NY: Springer.

Gunn, K. S., Trembath, D., & Hudry, K. (2014). An examination of interactions among children with autism and their typically developing peers. *Developmental Neurorehabilitation, 17*(5), 327-338.

Harvey, E. A., Lugo-Candelas, C. I., Breaux, R. P. (2015) Longitudinal changes in individual symptoms across the preschool years in children with ADHD. *Journal of Clinical Child and Adolescent Psychology, 44*(4), 580–594.

Hattie, J. (2008). *Visible learning: A synthesis of over 800 meta-analyses relating to achievement.* Abingdon-on-Thames, UK: Routledge.

Hazlett, H. C., Gu, H., Munsell, B. C., Kim, S. H., Styner, M., Wolff, J. J., ... & Collins, D. L. (2017). Early brain development in infants at high risk for autism spectrum disorder. *Nature, 542*(7641), 348-351.

Hellendoom, A., Langstraat, I., Wijnroks, L., Buitelaar, J. K., van Daalen, E., & Leseman, P. P. M. (2014). The relationship between atypical visual processing and social skills in young children with autism. *Research in Developmental Disabilities, 35*(2), 423-428.

Heinrichs, B. (2005). *Perfect targets: Asperger syndrome and bullying: Practical solutions for surviving the social world.* Shawnee Mission, KS: AAPC Publishing.

Henry, S. A., & Myles, B. S. (2013). *The Comprehensive Autism Planning System (CAPS) for individuals with autism spectrum disorders and related disabilities integrating evidence-based practices throughout the student's day* (2nd ed.). Future Horizons.

Hestenes, L. L., & Carroll, D. E. (2000). The play interactions of young children with and without disabilities: Individual and environmental influences. *Early Childhood Research Quarterly, 15*(2), 229-246.

Hodgetts, S., & Park, E. (2017). Preparing for the future: A review of tools and strategies to support autonomous goal setting for children with youth with autism spectrum disorders. *Disability and Rehabilitation, 39*(6), 535-543.

Hudson, F. G., Colson, S. E., & Braxdale, C. T. (1984). Instructional planning for dysfunctional learners: Levels of presentation. *Focus on Exceptional Children, 17*(3), 1-12.

Huitt, W. (2011). Motivation to learn: An overview. In *Educational Psychology Interactive*. Valdosta, GA: Valdosta State University. Retrieved [date] from http://www.edpsycinteractive.org/topics/cognition/piaget.html.

IDEA 2004 Reauthorization [34 CFR 300.1(a)] [20 U.S.C. 1400(d)(1)(A)]. www.idea.ed.gov.

Jahr, E., Eikeseth, S., Eldevik, S., & Aase, H. (2007). Frequency and latency of social interaction in an inclusive kindergarten setting: A comparison between typical children and children with autism. *Autism, 11*(4), 349-363.

Jónsdóttir, S. L., Saemundsen, E., Antonsdóttir, I. S., Sigurdardóttir, S., & Ólason, D. (2011). Children diagnosed with autism spectrum disorder before or after the age of 6 years. *Research in Autism Spectrum Disorders, 5*(1), 175-184.

REFERENCES

Klein, M. (1990, September). The physics of J. Willard Gibbs in his time. *Physics Today, 43*(9), 40.

Klin, A., Danovitch, J. H., Merz, A. B., & Volkmar, F. R. (2007). Circumscribed interests in higher functioning individuals with autism spectrum disorders: An exploratory study. *Research & Practice for Persons With Severe Disabilities, 32*(2), 89-100.

Knapen, T., Brascamp, J., Pearson, J., van Ee, R., & Blake, R. (2011). The role of frontal and parietal brain areas in bistable perception. *Journal of Neuroscience, 31*(28), 10293-10301.

Koegel, R. L., & Mentis, M. (1985). Motivation in childhood autism: Can they or won't they. *Journal of Child Psychology and Psychiatry, 26*(2), 185-191.

Kohls, G., Schulte-Rüther, M., Nehrkorn, B., Müller, K., Fink, G. R., Kamp-Becker, I., ... & Konrad, K. (2012). Reward system dysfunction in autism spectrum disorders. *Social Cognitive and Affective Neuroscience*, nss033.

Lang, R., Koegel, L. K., Ashbaugh, K., Regester, A., Ence, W., & Smith W. (2010). Physical exercise and individuals with autism spectrum disorders. *Research in Autism Spectrum Disorders, 4*, 565-526.

Leekam, S. R., Neito, C., Libby, S. J., Wing, L., & Gould, J. (2007). Describing the sensory abnormalities of children and adults with autism. *Journal of Autism and Developmental Disorders, 37*, 894-910.

Leon-Geurrero, R., Matsumoto, C., & Martin, J. (2011). *Show me the data: Data-based instructional decisions made simple and easy.* Shawnee Mission, KS: AAPC Publishing.

Levin, J. E., & Miller, J. P. (1996). Broadband neural encoding in the cricket cereal sensory system enhanced by stochastic resonance. *Nature, 280*(6570), 165-168.

Locke, E., Shaw, K. N., Saari, L. M., & Latham, G. P. (1981). Goal setting and task performance: 1969-1980. *Psychological Bulletin.* doi:10.1037//0033-2909.90.1.125.

Long, N. J., Morse, W. C., & Newman, R. G. (1976). *Conflict in the classroom: The educational children with problems* (3rd ed.). Belmont, CA: Wadsworth.

Mataya, K., Aspy, R., & Shaffer, H. (2017). *Talk with me: A step-by-step conversation framework for teaching conversational balance and fluency.* Shawnee Mission, KS: AAPC Publishing.

Mataya, K., & Owens, P. (2013). *Successful problem solving for high-functioning students with autism spectrum disorder.* Shawnee Mission, KS: AAPC Publishing.

McCormick, M. P., & O'Connor, E. E. (2015). Teacher-child relationship quality and academic achievement in elementary school: Does gender matter? *Journal of Educational Psychology, 107*(2), 502-516.

Merriam-Webster. (2006). *The Merriam-Webster dictionary.* Springfield, MA: Author.

Michna, I., & Trestman, R. (2016). Correctional management and treatment of autism spectrum disorder. *Journal of the American Academy of Psychiatry Law, 44,* 253-258.

Miodovnik, A., Harstad, E., Sideridis, G., & Huntington, N. (2015). Timing of the diagnosis of attention-deficit/hyperactivity disorder and autism spectrum disorder. *Pediatrics, 136*(4), e830-e837.

Moss, F., Ward L. M., & Sannita W. G. (2004). Stochastic resonance and sensory information processing: A tutorial and review of application. *Clinical Neurophysiology, 115*(2), 267-81.

Munch, C. (2010, November 22). *Pushing an online business to gain momentum.* Retrieved from http://munchweb.com/the-tipping-point.

Murray, C., & Malmgren, K. (2005). Implementing a teacher–student relationship program in a high-poverty urban school: Effects on social, emotional, and academic adjustment and lessons learned. *Journal of School Psychology, 43*(2), 137-152.

Myles, B. S. (2005). *Children and youth with Asperger Syndrome: Strategies for success in inclusive settings.* Thousand Oaks, CA: Corwin.

Myles, B. S., & Aspy, R. (2016). *High-functioning autism and difficult moments: Practical solutions for meltdowns.* Shawnee Mission, KS: AAPC Publishing.

Myles, B. S., Mahler, K., & Robbins, L. A. (2014). *Sensory issues and high-functioning autism spectrum and related disorders: Practical solutions for making sense of the world* (2nd ed.). Shawnee Mission, KS: AAPC Publishing.

National Autism Center. (2009). *National standards report: Addressing the need for evidence-based practice guidelines for autism spectrum disorders.* Randolph, MA: Author.

National Autism Center. (2015). *Findings and conclusions: National standards project, Phase 2: Addressing the need for evidence-based practice guidelines for autism spectrum disorder.* Randolph, MA: Author.

National Professional Development Center on Autism Spectrum Disorders. (2009). *Evidence based practice briefs.* Retrieved from http://autismpdc.fpg.unc.edu/content/briefs.

National Professional Development Center on Autism Spectrum Disorder. (2015). *Evidence based practice briefs.* Retrieved from http://autismpdc.fpg.unc.edu/content/briefs.

National Technical Assistance Center on Transition. (n.d.). Improving postsecondary outcomes for all students with disabilities. Retrieved August 1, 2017 from http://transitionta.org.

O'Connor, E. E., Collins, B. A., & Supplee, L. (2012). Behavior problems in late childhood: The roles of early maternal attachment and teacher–child relationship trajectories. *Attachment & Human Development, 14*(3), 265-288.

Oliver, P., Marwell, G., & Teixeira, R. (1985). Theory of critical mass. I: Interdependence, group heterogeneity, and the production of collective action. *American Journal of Sociology, 91*(3), 522-556.

Ormrod, J. E. (2008). *Educational psychology: Developing learners.* Boston, MA:

Pearson Allyn Bacon Prentice Hall. Retrieved from http://www.education. com/reference/article/motivation-affects-learning-behavior/.

Orsmond, G. I., & Kuo, H. (2011). The daily lives of adolescents with an autism spectrum disorder: Discretionary time use and activity partners. *Autism, 15*, 1–21.

P21: Partnership for 21st Century Learning. (n.d.). *P21 framework for 21st learning*. Retrieved from http://www.p21.org/index.php.

Prizant, B. M., Wetherby, A. M., Rubin, E., Laurent, A. C., & Rydell, P. J. (2007). *The SCERTS Model: A comprehensive educational approach for children with autism spectrum disorder*. Baltimore, MD: Brookes.

Reeve, C., & Kabot, S. (2015). *Taming the data monster: Collecting and analyzing classroom data to improve student progress*. Shawnee Mission, KS: AAPC Publishing.

Richtel, M. (2010, August 15). Outdoors and out of reach: Studying the brain. *The New York Times*. Retrieved from http://www.nytimes. com/2010/08/16/technology/16brain.html?_r=1&pagewanted=all&.

Rimm-Kaufman, S. E., Pianta, R. C., Early, D. M., Cox, M. J., Saluja, G., Bradley, R. H, & Payne, C. (2002). Early behavioral attributes and teachers' sensitivity as predictors of competent behavior in the kindergarten classroom. *Journal of Applied Developmental Psychology, 23*, 451-470.

Robertson, K., Chamberlain, B., & Kasari, C. (2003). General education teachers' relationships with included students with autism. *Journal of Autism and Developmental Disorders, 33*(2), 123-130.

Rogers, E. (2003). *Diffusion of innovations*. New York, NY: Simon & Schuster.

Roux, A. M., Shattuck, P. T., Rast, J. E., Rava, J. A., & Anderson, K. A. (2015). *National autism indicators report: Transition into young adulthood*. Philadelphia, PA: Drexel University, A. J. Drexel Autism Institute, Life Course Outcomes Research Program.

Salazar, F., Baird, G., Chandler, S., Tseng, E., O'Sullivan, T., Howlin, P., Pickles, A., & Simonoff, E. (2015). Co-occurring psychiatric disorders in preschool and elementary school-aged children with autism spectrum disorder. *Journal of Autism and Developmental Disorders, 45*, 2283-2294.

Schipul, S. E., & Just, M. A. (2016). Diminished neural adaptation during implicit learning in autism. *Neuroimage, 125*, 332-341.

Schlieder, M. (2007). *With open arms: Creating school communities of support for kids with social challenges using circle of friends, extracurricular activities, and learning teams*. Shawnee Mission, KS: AAPC Publishing.

Simmons, D., & Milne, E. (2014). Response to Davis and Plaisted-Grant: Low or high endogenous neural noise in autism spectrum disorder? *Autism*. doi: 10.1177/1362361314557683.

Stewart, R. (1996). *Motivating students who have autism spectrum disorders*. Retrieved from https://www.iidc.indiana.edu/pages/Motivating-Students-Who-Have-Autism-Spectrum-Disorders.

Stoner, R., Chow, M. L., Boyle, M. P., Sunkin, S. M., Mouton, P. R., Roy, S., ... & Courchesne, E. (2014). Patches of disorganization in the neocortex of children with autism. *New England Journal of Medicine, 370*(13), 1209-1219.

Vermeulen, P. (2012). *Autism as context blindness.* Shawnee Mission, KS: AAPC Publishing.

Vroom, V. H. (1964). *Work and motivation.* New York, NY: John Wiley & Sons.

Vygotsky, L. S. (1978). *Mind in society: The development of higher psychological functions.* Cambridge, MA: Harvard University Press.

Walker, C. M., & Gopnik, A. (2014). Toddlers infer higher-order relational principles in causal learning. *Psychological Science, 25*(1), 161-169.

Wayne, D. B., Butter, J., Siddall, V. J., Fudala, M. J., Wade, L. D., Feinglass, J., & McGaghie, W. C. (2006). Mastery learning of advanced cardiac life support skills by internal medicine residents using simulation technology and deliberate practice. *Journal of General Internal Medicine, 21*(3), 251-256.

Wiggins, G. (2012). Seven keys to effective feedback. *Educational Leadership, 70*(1), 10-16.

Wilde, L. D., Koegel, L. K., & Koegel, R. L. (1992). *Increasing success in school through priming: A training manual.* Santa Barbara, CA: University of California.

Wilhelm, T. (2009). The smallest chemical reaction system with bistability. *BMC Systems Biology, 3*(1), 90.

Winter-Messiers, M. A. (2007). Toilet brushes and tarantulas: Understanding the origin and development of special interest areas in children and youth with Asperger's syndrome. *Journal of Remedial and Special Education, 28*(3), 140-152.

Winter-Messiers, M. A., Herr, C. M., Wood, C. E., Brooks, A. P., Gates, M. A. M., Houston, T. L., & Tingstad, K. I. (2007). How far can Brian ride the Daylight 4449 Express? A strength-based model of Asperger syndrome based on special interest areas. *Focus on Autism and Other Developmental Disabilities, 22*(2), 67-79.

Wolfberg, P., Bottema-Beutel, K., & DeWitt, M. (2012). Including children with autism in social and imaginary play with typical peers: Integrated play groups model. *American Journal of Play, 5*(1), 55.

Wong, C., Odom, S. L., Hume, K. A., Cox, C. W., Fettig, A., Kurcharczyk, S., et al. (2015). Evidence-based practices for children, youth, and young adults with autism spectrum disorder: A comprehensive review. *Journal of Autism and Developmental Disorders, 45*(7), 1951-1966.

Worster, W. T. (2013). The transformation of quantity into quality: Critical mass in the formation of customary international law. *Boston University International Law Journal, 31*(1), 1-78.

Zeeland, S. V., Ashley, A., Dapretto, M., Ghahremani, D. G., Poldrack, R. A., & Bookheimer, S. Y. (2010). Reward processing in autism. *Autism Research, 3*(2), 53-67.

APPENDIX: INTERVENTIONS

Cartooning

Cartooning is a generic term that is used to describe the drawing educational professionals do to explain situations, events, or language terms (such as idioms or metaphors) to their clients. Cartooning strategies were refined by Arwood and Brown (1999) in their book, *A Guide to Cartooning and Flowcharting: See the Ideas.* The cartoon is used to: (a) explain and change behavior, (b) improve social skills, (c) manage time, and (d) improve academic skills. Also using cartoons, Gray (1994) introduced Comic Strip Conversations™ to illustrate and interpret social situations.

Arwood, E. L., & Brown, M. M. (1999). *A guide to cartooning and flowcharting: See the ideas.* Portland, OR: Apricot.
Gray, C. (1994). *Comic strip conversations: Colorful, illustrated interactions with students with autism and related disorders.* Jenison, MI: Jenison Public Schools.

Mapping

Mapping is a visual strategy that illustrates sequences of events, timelines, cause/effect, choice making, others' thoughts and actions, antecedent/behavior/consequence, prediction, and so forth. Mapping can be used to teach and support academic, social, daily living, recreational, and vocational skills (Buie, 2013).

Buie, A. (2013). *Behavior mapping: A visual strategy for teaching appropriate behavior to individuals with autism spectrum and related disabilities.* Shawnee Mission, KS; AAPC Publishing.

The Power Card Strategy

Based on a child's special interest, The Power Card Strategy (Gagnon & Myles, 2016) contains two components: (a) a text-based scenario that describes a behavior associated with a person's special interest and how that individual addresses that behavior, and encourages the child to use the strategy employed by the person of special interest; and (b) a small card that synthesizes the text-based scenario. Pictures of the special interest are often included on the scenario and the Power Card, itself.

Gagnon, E., & Myles, B. S. (2016). *The Power Card Strategy 2.0: Using special interests to motivate children and youth with autism spectrum disorder.* Shawnee Mission, KS: AAPC Publishing.

The Problem-Solving Rubric

Created for use in home, school, and community, the Problem Solving Rubric is designed to help learners understand cause and effect, problem solving, and decision-making. Building on the visual strengths of individuals on the spectrum, this strategy is effective for individuals from elementary-school age through adulthood (Mataya & Owens, 2013).

Mataya, K. & Owens, P. (2013). *Successful problem-solving for high-functioning students with autism spectrum disorder.* Shawnee Mission, KS: AAPC Publishing.

T-Charts

T-charts are a helpful way of depicting contrasting information such as "kind/un-kind words," "things you say to teachers/peers," and "home/school topics." The chart can be amended as new skills are learned or as new incidents arise.

Aspy, R., & Grossman, B. (2011). T*he Ziggurat Model: A framework for designing comprehensive interventions for high-functioning individuals with autism spectrum disorders.* Shawnee Mission, KS: AAPC Publishing.

Travel Card

The Travel Card, first discussed by Jones and Jones (1995), is designed to (a) increase productive behavior in adolescents with ASD across their many environments, (b) facilitate collaboration between teachers, (c) increase awareness among teachers of the goals the student is working on, and (d) improve home-school communication. Using the Travel Card, teachers monitor four to five target behaviors across classes and student student accumulates points that can be exchanged for reinforcers.

Carpenter, L. (2002). The travel card. In B. S. Myles & D. Adreon (Eds.), *Asperger Syndrome and adolescence: Practical solutions for school success* (pp. 92-96). Shawnee Mission, KS: AAPC Publishing.

Video Modeling

Video modeling typically involves taping adults, children or a target learner engaging in specific behaviors. The learner subsequently watches the video several times and is then observed to see if he can demonstrate the target behaviors.

Aspy, R., & Grossman, B. (2011). T*he Ziggurat Model: A framework for designing interventions comprehensive interventions for high-functioning individuals with autism spectrum disorders.* Shawnee Mission, KS: AAPC Publishing.

Visual Supports

Visual supports, such as pictures, written schedules, or even cartoon strips, use words, symbols, and pictures to address a variety of needs, including increased predictability and explanation of social situations. Furthermore, they can serve to break down a task into a series of steps (task analysis) to be followed one at a time. This facilitates independence in areas, such as daily living skills, social skills and academic tasks.

Aspy, R., & Grossman, B. (2011). *The Ziggurat Model: A framework for designing interventions comprehensive interventions for high-functioning individuals with autism spectrum disorders.* Shawnee Mission, KS: AAPC Publishing.

Social Narratives

Social narratives provide support and instruction for children and adolescents with AS who engage in interactions by describing social cues and appropriate responses to social behavior and teaching new social skills. Written at the child's instructional level, and often using pictures or photographs to confirm content, social narratives can promote self-awareness, self-calming, and self-management. There are several types of social narratives: descriptive stories; Social Stories™ (Gray, 1994); social scripts; cartooning (Arwood & Brown, 1999); the Power Card strategy (Gagnon & Myles, 2016); and Situation, Options, Consequences, Choices, Strategies, Simulation (SOCCSS; Roosa, cited in Myles & Adreon, 2001).

Arwood, E. L., & Brown, M. M. (1999). *A guide to cartooning and flowcharting: See the ideas.* Portland, OR: Apricot.

Gagnon, E., & Myles, B. S. (2016). *The Power Card Strategy 2.0: Using special interests to motivate children and youth with autism spectrum disorder.* Shawnee Mission, KS: AAPC Publishing.

Gray, C. (1994). *Comic Strip Conversations™: Colorful, illustrated interactions with students with autism and related disorders.* Jenison, MI: Jenison Public Schools.

Myles, B. S., & Adreon, D. (2001). *Asperger Syndrome and adolescence: Practical solutions for school success.* Shawnee Mission, KS: AAPC Publishing.

More from Future Horizons!

Flipp the Switch 2.0 provides educators with detailed information about executive function skills and evidence-based practices that can be used with students with autism spectrum disorder who experience executive function (EF) deficits to be more successful in school, at home, in the community, and in the future.

Carol Burmeister, Sheri Wilkins and Rebecca Silva

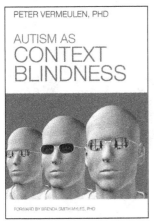

Dr. Vermeulen has produced a brilliant work that demands attention. *Autism as Context Blindness* provides a unique glance into the minds of individuals with autism. A Mom's Choice Award winner, it provides a unique glance into the minds of individuals with autism. It is simple but ground-breaking.

Peter Vermeulen

Broccoli Boot Camp is a comprehensive guide for parents of children who are selective or picky eaters, and can be used with children with or without special needs (e.g, autism or Down syndrome). It presents commonsense behavioral interventions to successfully expand children's diet variety and preferences for healthy foods.

Keith E. Williams and Laura Seiverling

Printed in the USA
CPSIA information can be obtained
at www.ICGtesting.com
JSHW010015220923
48851JS00004B/4